GIRDED
WITH
STRENGTH

A Story of Trial and Truimph

by

Viola Weidemann

Girded With Strength

All biblical quotations are from the Authorized King James
Version of the Bible, unless otherwise indicated.

Published by:

The McDougal Publishing Company
P.O. Box 3595
Hagerstown, MD 21742-3595

ISBN 1-884369-13-8

Printed in the United States of America
For worldwide distribution

For thou wilt light my candle: the Lord my God will enlighten my darkness.

For by thee I have run through a troop; and by my God have I leaped over a wall.

As for God, his way is perfect: the word of the Lord is tried: he is a buckler to all those that trust in him.

For who is God save the Lord? or who is a rock save our God?

***It is God that GIRDETH ME WITH STRENGTH**, and maketh my way perfect.*   Psalm 18:28-32

Dedication

He sent from above, he took me, he drew me out of
many waters.   **Psalm 18:16**

With deep and everlasting love this book is dedicated
to the Lord Jesus Christ, the Shepherd of my soul and the
love of my life.

Contents

About the Cover

*For thou wilt light my candle: the LORD my God
will enlighten my darkness.* Psalm 18:28

When I first saw the photograph I have used for the
cover of my book, I thought how much like uncharted
seas our life is. But through it is a shining path — a reflec-
tion of God's constant presence, His sure plan for us, and
the warmth of His Great Love, guiding us homeward.

Introduction

In the lives of all the people of the Bible, the great signal fires were the meetings they had with God, the times that God came to them and manifested His presence to them. Even when men and women seemed to be initiating such encounters themselves, it was God who made the first step. Jesus said:

> *No man can come to me, except the Father which hath sent me draw him.*   John 6:44

The people of the Bible were ordinary until the touch of God came upon them. His touch was the common denominator between male and female, rich and poor, gifted and common. It is His touch that turns the ordinary into the extraordinary, the profane into the holy.

In every person's life, sets of circumstances — happenings for good or for evil — trigger a great desire in us to have fellowship with God, to meet with Him, to know Him, to see what He is thinking and to see what He wants to say to us. Our response at these moments determines the future course of our lives.

My prayer is that as you read the pages of this book you will be challenged to seek God in a greater way so that you can be turned into another person by His power and that He can make something wonderful of your life.

The only important thing in this life is not what one thinks or feels. It is always "What does God have to say about it?" When God speaks and His will is performed, then joy and peace can flourish.

Viola Weidemann
Ashland, Virginia

Chapter 1

The Foundation

He sent from above, he took me, he drew me out of many waters.   Psalm 18:16

The earliest memory I have of the Lord was when I was four or five years old. My parents usually sent me to Sunday School, although Mother sometimes went with me. Dressed in a little wide-brimmed sailor hat, my navy coat, my white gloves and my tiny little purse, I was sent half a block away to a marvelous Presbyterian church. I could hear the music from my house. There were trumpets, there were trombones, the organ, the piano and guitars. An excitement would build in my little heart as I went toward the sound of the music.

I remember well my Sunday school teacher. She used flannel-graphs and, with all the usual drawings and gestures, made the Lord and the stories of the Bible real to me. At Christmas time, there was a manger scene under a tree in our classroom. I looked at it with fascination; and, when I got home, I asked my mother if I could have one too.

Mother was pleased, and that week she went to town and bought me a little manger scene. It consisted of a tiny, carved wooden figure of Baby Jesus in a little wooden manger with real straw in it and the figures of Mary and Joseph, a little donkey, a cow and a camel. I knelt down under the tree in the evening while Mother was washing the dishes in the kitchen, and I felt overcome with love for that little baby in the manger.

I tenderly lifted the Baby from the manger and held Him. In that moment, I felt so in love with Him that I just popped Him into my mouth. Now, that may seem strange to many, but it was an experience that I have never forgotten in fifty-five years. The important thing was not the wooden figures but what was happening in my heart.

My earliest recollection of the salvation experience came a year or two later, when I was at my grandmother's house one day. Obviously I did something I shouldn't have, although I can't remember now what it was. My mother said to me, "That's a sin." That frightened me because my Sunday School teacher had told me that if you sinned, you couldn't go to Heaven — unless you asked Jesus to forgive you. So, up I went to the room in which we were staying in my grandmother's house, and I knelt down and cried, sobbing, "Lord Jesus, forgive me of all my sins," and He did. It was just as simple as that.

All of a sudden, instead of crying, I felt like laughing. All of a sudden, instead of feeling so alone, I felt the Lord standing there beside me. Although I couldn't see Him with my eyes, I could certainly see Him with my heart, and at last I knew what it meant to be forgiven. At last I knew, in experience, what my Sunday school teacher and Aunt Catherine (my grandfather's sister who was an ordained Baptist minister) had been telling me. I sometimes visited Aunt Catherine out in the Amish country, and each morning she knelt with me at my bedside and we prayed together.

Because Sunday school was only once each week, and because I didn't have friends at that age who came over to talk about God, I'm sure I didn't get as close to Him as I could have. When the days are sweet and the years seem to roll carelessly by, and you have wonderful parents and grandparents and lovely grass lawns to play on, and life seems free of trouble, I suppose you don't really seek the Lord like you should. I continued to attend Sunday school every Sunday, but I can't remember other significant visits from the Lord — until I was about nine years old.

Something terrible happened when I was nine, terrible as far as our family was concerned. One day, without warning, mother told me that Father was leaving and that they were getting a "divorce." I couldn't understand the "why" of this, of course. Maybe no one ever does, especially a child. I ran up to my room where I always talked to the Lord and looked at my *Hurlbut's Story of the Bible* that Mother had given to me even before I learned to read well. I had loved its pictures and remember finding that same picture of the Baby Jesus in the manger and of rubbing that page with my hand and loving Him in my heart.

Now, I ran crying to my bedroom and prayed, "Lord, my father's leaving. You're going to have to be my father." Suddenly, the entire room filled with glory, and I heard Him speak. He said, "I will be, but when you want to know something, I want you to come to My Word. I want you to be a good girl, be a good daughter, and don't let anyone ever say of you, in pity, 'That poor child! She's from a broken home.' Your home is not broken. I am your Father." In that moment, a great peace filled my heart.

In the years that followed, I often met with the Lord — in Sunday school, in my room and through reading my Bible. My Bible now became a lifeline to Heaven, a lifeline to wisdom, a lifeline to correction, to edification, to God's character.

I remember a time when I was frustrated, not knowing how to pray. I sensed the Lord telling me to read the Psalms. I sat down with the Psalms in front of me. The Lord said, "Now, read them out loud to Me as though you wrote them yourself." As I obeyed, I felt a new liberty in prayer that I had never experienced before.

The Psalms are not just praise. They are filled with instruction, with teaching; and, through reading them, we can look straight into the character of Jesus. Thus, we learn how to ask God for things that He wants us to have, and we learn what pleases Him. That is what I wanted to do more than anything else in the world.

My mother followed the Bible principle that when a woman is so unfortunate as to be divorced, *"let her be returned to her father's house."* She took my sister and me to live with her parents, our grandparents.

Mother is well educated and a lovely and wonderful person. She was accustomed to fine things and accustomed to gentle treatment. Why should anyone in that position, and with daughters to raise, be scratching around in some lesser job, or be raising those daughters in some cramped apartment across town, in a bad neighborhood? Too many women live in these reduced circumstances and have no one to care for their children. This is a modern-day tragedy. Mother did the scriptural thing in going home to an honorable father's house and slipped right back into the loveliness of her parents' care and the protection of her father's good name. Women who find themselves in such circumstances would do well to follow her example.

Grandfather was a well-known manufacturer. In his house, we had love and safety. We received a good education in the loving arms of the father and patriarch of our own family. What could be more wonderful? If more women followed this biblical counsel they wouldn't be living independently just for the sake of "doing their own thing," or for the sake of rebelling against their parents.

"No one is going to tell me what to do" is the attitude of most women today. Some say, "I am a grown woman, and it is time for me to have my own life. Mama is not going to tell me what to do from now on." There is so much rebellion and selfishness in people nowadays that divorced women often find themselves in the position of being put at risk by predatory men or by a life-style that leads to sin and the decimation of the family and even to the molestation of their own children by neighbors or by a boyfriend. God is not pleased with this.

Living with my grandparents, nevertheless, was a bittersweet experience. There was sadness in my heart that my father was gone, but my heavenly Father stepped into the breach and became all things to me. I was still very young and needed to learn how to approach God, how to speak with Him. I had to learn how to pull down healing for myself, how to have my thinking adjusted to His. In all of this, He was faithful. The Holy Ghost is totally capable of rearing a child.

When you are born-again, it isn't long before you offend or anger someone else in the family. One day at the breakfast table I said, concerning the subject of conversation, "The Bible says ... ." Every head turned my way, and one member of the family asked, "Can't you ever talk about anything except God?"

I concealed my hurt as best I could, but as soon as breakfast had ended, I went right to my room, to my meeting place with God, and I said to Him, with a trembling lip and much self-pity, "Lord, they don't love me."

I didn't have to wait long for His reply. I felt that marvelous presence again, and I heard Him speak. He said, "It's not you, it's Me."

God doesn't need to speak volumes to make us understand what He means. Then and there, I understood that I could not have a martyr complex, that I could not feel self-pity, and I understood something else that has kept me strong all these years. I was not about to give up God because others found Him offensive in me. I was sorry that they felt that way, but I would not give Him up – for anyone or anything.

"Would you go through some other things like this with Me," He asked, "if you knew that while enduring this pain and these hurts some day all your victories would serve as good lessons for other people?"

I remember saying to Him, "Yes, Lord." I believe that when you say *yes* to the Lord it is an eternal *yes*. I said *yes* then, and today I say *yes* still.

A year or two later, I remember looking through the Bible, reading and praying. There is something called "pray reading." As you read, when the Spirit makes something real, and God is about to make another covenant with your life, all of a sudden there is a feeling that you want to weep. The Bible becomes so real, and that passage of Scripture leaps out at you, as it were. At that point, I always stop to worship and pray.

On this particular day, I felt the presence of God as I was reading the story of Solomon. As I read what God was speaking to Solomon, suddenly God stepped off the pages of that Word, and said to me, as He had to Solomon, "*Ask what I shall give thee*" (See 1 Kings 3:5 and 2 Chronicles 1:7).

That was so great a word, such a marvelous meeting with Him, that the fear of God overtook me, and I felt within myself that I had better search through the Bible to see what God wanted me to ask of Him. I knew that this was a momentous occasion.

I had no sooner begun to search when my eyes fell on the words, "*Give thy servant an understanding heart*" (1 Kings 3:5). I began to see that everything God spoke to His servants in the Bible He wants to speak to us too. All the marvelous covenants He made with His people in Bible days He wants to make with us, as well. As He appeared to them, He wants to appear to us. As He spoke with them, He wants to speak with us. That knowledge thrilled me, and I felt the great power of God weighing heavily upon my spirit. I said to Him, "Lord, give me an understanding heart."

I felt His mighty presence, and He said, "I have."

Then, it seemed as if He slowly went out of the room. Our encounter was over. He had beckoned me to ask something, I had discovered what to ask and had done it, and I felt that God and I had made a covenant that day.

When I was twelve, my mother remarried, and we moved to another neighborhood. My new stepfather was an employee of Grandfather's and a well-to-do man in his own right; but, alas, he did not communicate with children. I wanted so much to be a good daughter and to be pleasing and helpful to adults, but no one could get close to him. It wasn't long before we discovered that he was an alcoholic. It was personally very hurtful to me because I had never seen anyone drunk in my life. To live in the house with a drunkard was a great test. Day after day, I heard God tell me, as others were disenchanted with the man and his behavior, "I have saved you for this hour. I have caused you to have My Spirit in you. You must be kind to him."

From that time on, instead of shrinking from the presence of the man, as I sat in the room trembling because of the smell of alcohol, I opened myself to God and allowed Him to put kind words in my heart and in my mouth, to answer questions about that Bible that my stepfather had. I remember travailing in prayer for him and weeping over his soul. While he would never talk to others about the Bible, he often said to me, "It is amazing how you can see these things and others can't." I give all the glory to God. I can't say that he was ever saved, but he was one of the great challenges of my life, and I did what I could to win him. (We cannot force men and women to God, only to live godly lives before them and to be sure they see the way of salvation.) In all of this, I grew closer and closer to Jesus.

When we first moved into that new community, I attended the Presbyterian church, but I went home and wept. Most of the people were not born-again. Even the pastor seemed cold. I didn't know enough at the time to even use the term *born-again*, but I knew that I could not feel the presence of the Lord in that place, as I had in my former church.

I wept as I prayed, "Help me, Lord. I need a place to continue growing in Your love and people who love You with whom I can fellowship." Soon after that, a new friend at school invited me to go with her to her church. It was an Episcopalian church and it was my first time to attend a church of that denomination. I felt surprisingly at home there. As I knelt for the first time in the church, it was just like kneeling at home. A mystical love for Jesus washed over me. When I saw the people taking the Holy Communion and reverencing the cross of Christ, when I saw the priest bowing at the altar, and when I heard the beauty of the hymns, tears coursed down my face. I felt Jesus in this new place, and I was about to learn the mystical loveliness of worship in the Episcopalian ritualistic concept.

During the coming years, I got in the habit of going into the church on my way home from school and praying. Sometimes I would return to the church at night. If no one was present, I would kneel on the marble altar where only the priest stood at service times and, feeling a closeness of the Lord, I began to sense a new calling on my life.

After I graduated from high school, I began to attend a well-known art institute for women which my mother had attended before me. I felt a new surge of fulfillment as I began to use and develop the natural artistic talents that God had given me.

Chapter 2

My Life As Wife and Young Mother

As for God, his way is perfect: the word of the Lord is tried: he is a buckler to all those that trust in him.

Psalm 18:30

When I was nineteen I felt a great presence of the Lord in my bedroom one night as I sought Him in prayer. Responding to His presence, I laid myself on the floor in front of Him and opened my heart.

"Lord," I said, "It is about time for me to be married, but I don't know anyone I want to marry. Let me never be divorced. I know people who have made terrible mistakes in their marriages and who have lived lives of terrible hurt from that moment on. Please help me!"

I felt so strongly about the sanctity of marriage that I made a vow that day, a vow for which I have always been grateful. "Lord, I will not marry unless You choose my husband."

I heard His voice, saying: "I will, but stop dating."

That was a new concept to me, but God had been a faithful Father to me for many years. Why should I not trust Him now? I broke off all my friendships with young men and refrained from going out to dinner or driving with them.

A month or two passed, and one day I went to buy a winter coat at a nearby department store. I was trying on a coat when I saw a white-haired lady sitting in a chair, with her purchases in her lap, looking at me.

"Is your name Viola?" she asked.

"Yes," I answered.

"Don't you remember me?" she said. "I'm Mrs. Weidemann. You used to live two doors away from us when you were a child."

I looked closely, and then I remembered her.

"I have two boys. Remember?" she said. "You used to play together." She named the boys. "Let me take your phone number home," she continued. "I am sure they would love to see you again."

That night the phone rang. It was Mrs. Weidemann's oldest son calling. He wanted to see me, he said. Since God had told me not to date and that He would choose my husband, I answered him, "I'm sorry. I remember the good times we had together while we were young, but I can't go out on a date."

"Please," he said, "I broke another date to see you. I was so excited when mother came home and said she had seen you again. I would really love to see you after so many years."

"I can't go out," I insisted.

"Well, could I come there?" he said.

"Well, I suppose it would be all right, but my grand-mother's here, and we're not to go anywhere."

"That's fine," he assured me.

In about forty-five minutes, I heard his car approach-ing, heard his footsteps up the stone steps, and heard his knock at the door. I went to the door and, as I opened it, something very strange happened. I had the most amazing feeling, as if I had been kicked in the mid section by a mule. As the door opened, and I saw the man whom I hadn't seen since I was eight or nine years old, God said to me, "Here is your husband."

It was just that simple: a husband, chosen surely by the Lord. I wasn't in love, I thought, yet I had heard God speak.

He came in, and we talked about many things. Within ten days, we were in love with God's choice, and I had the Weidemann family engagement ring on my finger. A year later Warren and I were married.

After we met, I took him to my pastor at the Episcopalian Church in Philadelphia (which I attended because it was near my college dormitory). He counseled us both, finding us with faith in Jesus, and he put us both into a confirmation class together.

We had a large and wonderful wedding presided over by our pastor who preached the Gospel every Sunday on the radio. The night before the wedding, I lay in bed and lifted my hands to the Lord and said, "Lord Jesus, be there tomorrow and marry us, and let everyone feel Your presence." As I went up that long aisle in Holy Trinity Church in Philadelphia and met my groom at the altar, the love and power of God was felt by everyone.

At the end of the service, the minister took his surplice and bound it around our hands, and we could feel the presence of the Lord. The wedding guests later commented that they felt the presence of God in that place. It was so remarkable that the following day the pastor spoke on the subject of God's love and presence and our wedding. We thus began a happy married life.

Within the next six years, we had four children, all

daughters. I had always loved children and looked forward to being a mother; but now I found that being
responsible for such dear creatures was a great and joyful
challenge. I had to ask God for His help every day. I was
no longer under the protection of my family. I was an
adult with adult responsibilities. I had to adjust to life
with a husband and adjust to being a mother. I had been
thrust forth from the nest, and I needed God's help.

Every baby brought me closer to God. I nursed them all
and, at two in the morning, when I was there alone with
my child and my God, rocking in the chair, I would sing
the words to every hymn I had ever learned; and the tears
would run freely down my face. I wanted to be everything God wanted me to be, not only for Him, but also to
be a good example for the girls. My highest goal in life
was to be a good wife and a good mother. As my responsibilities grew, my spirit softened, as I sought the Lord's
help.

I had my last child the summer my husband graduated
from law school. Not long after that our pastor asked me
if I would paint a centerpiece for the children's altar of the
church, a tryptic of three panels of wood, made in the
medieval style. (By this time, my husband and I were both
Sunday school teachers in the Episcopalian Church in the
suburbs of Philadelphia.) On the left panel I painted ani-
mals of the world and, on the right, all the children of the
world. I used models or photographs for some of the
work that I did, but for the centerpiece, the Virgin Mary
holding the Baby Jesus, I painted my heart into it. In the
Virgin's face, I put all my love for the children that God
had given me and all my love for the Baby Jesus; and into
the face of the Baby Jesus I painted all my devotion. I was
amazed to find that I could paint by the inspiration of the

Holy Spirit better than I had ever painted anything before or since, and I prayed for inspiration as I painted.

When I was finished with the Virgin and the Baby, I painted the dove of the Holy Spirit over them both. That week I asked God with all my heart to fill me with the Holy Spirit. Within the next few months, in my own house, seeking Him vigorously with prayer and fasting, and without ever having heard the term Pentecostal, I received the Holy Ghost. I began to speak in an ancient language that sounded to me like Chinese. I was so joyful that I rolled on the floor laughing and crying, speaking in tongues for hours.

My entire life was changed by this experience. All the fullness of the Godhead seemed to burst in upon me, and I enjoyed the Lord as I had never enjoyed Him before, I loved Him as I had never loved Him before, I appreciated Him like I had never appreciated Him before. I was thrilled to the bottom of my soul with Him. I entered a rich new period in the Word, a period in which I read voraciously and, suddenly, the mysteries of the Word of God began to become clear to me. Everything seemed to come into focus.

My fellowship was also greatly enhanced. Soon I began to meet, for the first time in my life, other Christians, mostly Episcopalians who were filled with the Holy Spirit. They were very dedicated Christians and shared the same zeal for the Lord. We met in prayer meetings and explored together the passages concerning the gifts of the Spirit. About this time, I learned more about fasting and about prayer in the Spirit, and a whole new world of prayer and crying out to God opened up to me, with speaking in tongues for hours at a time. It wasn't long before others began to recognize the power of God in my life. Soon, I was not only speaking in tongues, but also giving messages in tongues in the meetings, and, eventually, prophecy. I was also ministering to others outside the prayer groups. Whenever I could find free time, I would visit my lady friends and pray for them to receive the Holy Ghost.

I began to trust God for everything, for money beyond our income, for wisdom beyond my own and for understanding to raise the girls in God's ways. When my children were sick, I laid hands on them and, wonder of wonders, their fevers broke under my hands. Oh the joy of seeing the things of God become reality in my daily life!

Now, I felt the need to find a church that was Pentecostal. The gifts of the Spirit were not welcomed in the church I was attending, for the most part, and I was no longer satisfied to fellowship with those who wanted a halfway or partway experience with God. I was determined to identify with those who wanted the most they could get from Him, those who wanted the holiness I had seen in Christ in their own lives. It was that holiness that I desired for my own life and for the lives of my family members. I understood that I could not teach it to others if I could not live it myself, so I was dedicating myself fiercely to God everyday — my life, my mind, my spirit, my soul, my body, our money, our past, our present and our future.

I was attending a few charismatic meetings, but God showed me that I needed to find an "old fashioned" Pentecostal church. He told me, "Go where the pastors have been in this way for many years; go where men believe the whole Word of God; go where the people live a life of holiness; go and submit yourself to them." I found such a church, one of the oldest and most well-established Pentecostal churches in town and began to share with them my experience. Not long afterward I became a member of the church. I felt like I had put on the harness of the Holy Ghost at last. My pastor and his wife were old-timers who had come out of the Welsh Revival.

My husband, who had been until then a successful and brilliant research chemist, asked me what I thought about him going to Law school at night to become a patent attorney specializing in petrochemicals. It would take three years of very long days and much hard work and dedication. I could see that he was pressing into his career, so he had my blessing and help. In the long nights that followed that decision, I learned to pray in the Spirit with all my heart.

I never felt a conflict between family and ministry. With the birth of each of my daughters, I had also found greater fulfillment in life. Now, I did not feel that my serving the Lord was taking anything away from my husband or children, and I did not feel that, by being married or being a mother, I was losing anything or missing anything. I was not straining at the bit, called to do something without the members of my family. I was intent on fulfilling the plan of God for my life, and I knew that His plan included the man God had given me and the girls He had given me. I fasted intensively, and God filled my husband with the Spirit, and we went to church together as a family. Then, many evenings, with his permission, I was able to go with my lady friends to prayer meetings all over the city. There was no conflict between serving God and serving my family.

Although I was raised in a home of privilege and money and received a good education, one of the great concerns in our household was that each woman be a good wife and a good mother and that the women should not work outside the home after marriage, but only work for their husband and children. This was the thing to do in my family. I had been taught by a good mother, by good grandparents, and by good great-grandparents, and I was doing everything I knew to do to fulfill that tradition. I was trying to be the best wife I could be and the best mother I could be. At the same time I was learning to serve the Lord joyfully.

I always washed the girls' clothes happily and never complained about it or thought that task to be demeaning. As I hung out the clothes, I thanked God for the ability to hang them out, and I thanked Him for each of my children. I even made some of their clothing. When I was just learning with one of the girls, I loved my new baby so much that, not having a pattern for infant's clothes, I put the child down on the fabric, traced around her with a pen, and made her a little garment that way. It was finished by the end of the day. I will have to say that it was a little tight, but that dear little soul had a garment made by a loving mother.

I was a happy mother. I was loving God, and only by loving Him and appreciating Him can one be the best possible mother and wife. Those were wonderful days of contentment and joy for me. I was getting closer to God every day.

Chapter 3

An Ending and A Beginning

For thou wilt light my candle: the Lord my God will enlighten my darkness.　　　　　　　Psalm 18:28

As my husband became a more and more successful attorney, he began to acquire friends who were not very spiritual. Some were actually ungodly types. Not all his friends were from the petroleum company he worked for; he had met others. There were phone calls at night, from people wanting him to make investments or asking him for help or legal advice. Before long, he was keeping company with some clients that I instinctively knew were not good for him spiritually, men with hard faces and hard hearts.

As he made more money and was more successful, he began to slack off in church attendance and slack off in Bible reading. He could memorize entire passages of Scripture, something I found to be very difficult; but now he had no desire to do it. He could prophesy with much more power than I could; but now he seemed to be losing his appreciation for prophecy. I began to feel a chilling cloud coming over his life.

When I first noticed it, I began to fast and pray and hold on to God for him. Several years went by in this struggle, years in which I would weep before God, having my throat raw from interceding in tongues into the wee hours of the morning. There was nothing else I could do. When I saw this spiritual coldness descend over him, my defense was to cry out to God and to put myself on the line, as any intercessor who loves God and loves those for whom they are interceding. I threw myself into this struggle for my husband's soul. I began to pray as if Jesus would come that very night and find my husband unprepared. I stood in the gap in this way until I had no more strength to pray, no more strength to fast.

One night he was out for one of those interminable business meetings and, at midnight, I was still alone in my room. I took advantage of the time to read the Word and worship Jesus. Then, all of a sudden, that wondrous presence loomed very large in the room. The power of God Almighty filled that place, and my heart and soul were gripped in His awesome presence. I saw Jesus standing before me at the foot of the bed.

He put His hand out toward me, with love and all my future in His eyes, and He said, "Will you give me your joy for waters to swim in?" In that moment, I felt the fellowship of His suffering as I walked into my personal Gethsemane with Jesus. I wept and cried, and could hardly speak, my throat barely operating. After a time, I was able to cry out in tongues and pray out loud in English, "Lord Jesus, help me to say yes." Then, from the innermost part of my being (where, I am glad to say, He lives), came strength and power and victory, as always; and I cried out with all my heart, "Yes, Lord Jesus."

I thank my God that He turned off my mental facility at that moment so that I did not understand with my mind what was happening. I say this of Him Who is bound to show us the price at every turn; and He did show me the price; for, although I did not understand exactly what the Lord was saying, I could feel the heaviness of it. In myself, I could never have managed that YES; but, God, in my weakness, caused me to stand up and say YES, by His Spirit within me. One month later my husband suddenly and unexpectedly dropped dead while on a business trip out of state. There was no accident; he had no cancer; and there was no heart attack; he died on his knees in prayer! It happened twenty days before Christmas of 1970.

During those last weeks before my husband died, there were some strange events that I did not connect with imminent death, until later. Two Sundays before he passed into Heaven, he had said to me, "I don't want to go to church today, I want to bring the message to the family myself." I was thrilled and delighted, seeing that my prayers were taking hold. He came out of the bedroom where he studied and assembled the girls and me around the dining room table, and right there in our own home their father and my husband preached to us a wonderful message.

The last Sunday he spent on the Earth he repeated this amazing performance. When he had nearly finished speaking, he opened his Bible to Proverbs 31 and read that beautiful passage concerning the virtuous woman. He looked into my face and said, "You are that virtuous woman." My heart was strangely full.

As we closed that little service with prayer, he came around the table and laid his hands on each of us. When it came my turn to receive the laying on of his hands, I felt the weight of the patriarchal blessing pass from him to me. These would prove to be the last drops of his anointing flowing to us. Then strange silence.

That Friday night he left for a business trip in New York, to help another Christian brother. He was accompanied by another businessman. They were to spend the night in a motel in Rochester, New York, and meet with the preacher friend, for whom he was forming a company. (Philadelphia lawyers are well-known contract attorneys.) That afternoon I had been praying with a lady who was my prayer partner. As we knelt before the Lord, I saw a vision of feet walk over a threshold and a door open, and the feet go through the door, and bright glory stream in from the other side. I described to my friend what I had seen, and she said to me, "I have just seen the same thing."

At 9 a.m. on Saturday morning I was still in my bathrobe, preparing breakfast for my girls in the kitchen, when a knock came to the door. It was a state policeman with a clipboard in his hand. He asked me if I was Mrs. Weidemann and I said that I was. He said, "Ma'am, you had better sit down."

"I would rather stand," I answered. "Tell me one thing: Is he dead?"

"Yes," he replied.

I looked past the patrolman's head into Heaven and cried, "Hold me steady, Lord Jesus," and I felt my anchor go out and hit the Solid Rock.

There were tears, but they didn't come in a rush because now I caught sight of my girls, and they were in utter chaos, having overheard our conversation and not being at all prepared as I was for such a blow. I gathered them around me and consoled them. Then, as they went off screaming together, I knelt alone. The policeman stood watching, unable to understand such a scene. I called out loud, remembering the unfaithfulness of Job's wife, in their time of trouble. I bowed my face to the carpet and prayed, "Lord Jesus, I bow my neck under Thy will. Thou hast done perfectly by me. I worship and praise Thee."

All that day I had to be strong for those who came to console me. Each of them collapsed upon my shoulders and wept upon my neck. God lifted me up, and I felt angels' hands upon my arms and back and neck. Those who had pulled him into things that were not God's will for him came and stood with unseeing eyes, not knowing how they would fill the gap in their lives, in their companies, in their scheme of things; but my heart was exalted, and I said to God: "Safe, at last, from all the devil's power, safe this very hour."

That night, when the house was dark and everything was still, and the voices and the sobbings had ceased, and the girls were exhausted on their beds, I heard my Beloved's voice again. He said, "Was there ever a day that you could not praise Me?"

I said, "No, Lord," and took the tambourine and worshiped God in a dance in the darkened living room, with tears streaming down my face.

My husband's last words to me were: "I'll be home on the plane on Sunday night" — and so he was. On a cold, dark December night, his coffin was taken off that plane at the Philadelphia Airport.

The morning of the funeral, I heard the Lord speak to me. He said, "I want you to wear beige, not black. I want you to take off your wedding ring. The contract is broken. Your husband is dead." I found that my God is a total realist. He is truth itself. No custom that He does not author is allowed to take over.

"I want you to look forward and not back," He said.

"Do not put his picture before you any longer. Do not think of him, as he spoke to you in this way, or how he looked when he said that, and do not think of him in this room or that. What is ahead of you is a larger life. It is not a brick wall, it is a doorway to a bright future. You are Mine, and I am in control. I will lead you and guide you with Mine eye."

The afternoon of my husband's death, as I received those who came to console us, the Lord gave me all the Scriptures for the funeral. I spoke with the preacher about it because many of those who would be attending were unsaved, prominent lawyers and business people, and many of them had never attended a Pentecostal church. (People were to come from far away cities and drive in a funeral cortege that was two miles long.) There were Jewish friends that I had witnessed to for years, some of whom had served notice on me that they didn't want to hear any more about Jesus. There were relatives who scoffed at the blood of Jesus and denigrated our testimony. They were all there that day to hear a Pentecostal salvation message.

An elderly brother from our prayer group came to me and kissed me on the cheek. With tears streaming down his face, he said, "I saw your husband standing with Jesus in a vision this morning, on the other side of a bright river. He waved to me joyously and said, 'Kiss Viola for me.' "

As the casket slowly made its way out of the crowded funeral home, the organ could be heard echoing the glory strains of that old hymn of the church, *A Mighty Fortress Is Our God*:

> *A mighty fortress is our God,*
> *A bulwark never failing.*

Our Helper He amid the flood
Of mortal ills prevailing.   —Martin Luther

God was indeed my Fortress, and I was learning what it meant to live within the safety of His walls.

My girls were understandably devastated by the death of a father they deeply loved and respected. They needed to be brought back to life, so to speak. I sensed that nothing could serve that purpose better than reading to them about the beauties of Heaven. I had a wonderful book called *Intramuros* which contained testimonies of what Heaven is really like. For three days, we read together — morning, noon and night. They would not allow me to go to my room and leave them alone, fearing that I would be taken next. So, we sat together, around the Christmas tree, on quilts, and read and talked. Through the mighty witness of that book and through the working of the Holy Spirit through my words, the bruised spirits of the girls began to mend, and after three days, they were ready to face the future. I have read *Intramuros* regularly from that day on with great joy and anticipation of our heavenly home.

In the coming days and weeks, God did many miracles for us. There was a period of time, before the legal issues could be settled, that I could not take anything out of my own bank account. As a result, I had no money to feed the girls and was ashamed to tell anyone about it. Every night I set the table, putting the china and the silver out, and calling the girls; and every night the door bell rang and a different friend was there with something for us to eat. Jesus provides so wonderfully.

I was educated in the arts, in the languages, and in literature and domestic arts, and I had always hated

mathematics. Now, God showered me with wisdom and
helped me to close out my husband's estate in a very few
months. With the assistance of his law partner, everything was quickly taken care of. In record time, all the
loose ends were tied together. Just as the Lord knows
how to give a beautiful beginning to a life, He knows how
to close out a life on Earth — beautifully.

Chapter 4

Ashland, Virginia

*He brought me forth also into a large place; he deliv-
ered me, because he delighted in me.*   Psalm 18:19

As the months went by I sensed that my time in our
local church was coming to an end. I had always believed
that a woman should submit herself to strong spiritual
leadership, so I determined to take the girls and attend
the yearly conference at Elim Bible Institute in Rochester,
New York, a place that my husband and I had both loved
and visited for many years. The leaders of Elim were missionary men with a great vision and a dedicated life-style,
longtime friends of our pastor. We usually went up the
second week of July, but this time the Lord told me to go
the first week, so I got the plane tickets for that week
instead.

Once I had arrived at Elim, I made it known to the
leadership that I looked to them, as a new widow, to pray
for me and to take me under their wing, as it were. They
assured me that they would do just that.

I had some wonderful experiences at Elim. That year,

for instance, the Lord spoke to me one afternoon. I heard Him say, as though no time at all had elapsed since He had spoken to me many years before concerning the wisdom of Solomon, "Go up, sit down on your bed, and read the second part of the thing that I promised you."

I went up immediately and, with great expectancy, began to read. I found that when Solomon had said, *"Give therefore thy servant an understanding heart to judge thy people"* (1 Kings 3:9), God had answered that because Solomon had not asked for riches and honor, he would receive those as well:

> *And the speech pleased the Lord, that Solomon had asked this thing. And God said unto him, Because thou hast asked this thing, and hast not asked for thyself long life; neither hast asked riches for thyself, nor hast asked the life of thine enemies; but hast asked for thyself understanding to discern judgment; Behold, I have done according to thy words: lo, I have given thee a wise and an understanding heart; so that there was none like thee before thee, neither after thee shall any arise like unto thee. And I have also given thee that which thou hast not asked, both riches, and honour: so that there shall not be any among the kings like unto thee all thy days.*
>
> 1 Kings 3:10-13

I realized immediately that this was "the second part" of which God had spoken and that He was offering me the same thing that afternoon. I was overwhelmed with joy. Surely God was doing a new thing in my life. From that moment on, a new wisdom, new riches, and new honor settled upon me, such as I had never known.

That year the speaker for the first week was a lady missionary named Ruth Heflin from Calvary Pentecostal

Campground in Ashland, Virginia. The moment I saw her I felt the glory of God and the joy of the Lord. I felt something new was about to happen when I was around her, and we had wonderful fellowship together. As I spoke with her one day, I experienced something strange. I felt like I was falling forward, as if I would be slain in the Spirit at her feet.Toward the end of the week, she said to me, with a smile, "You must come down and attend our campmeeting next week."

"I've already been away from home and from my prayer group for a week," I protested.

"You come on the plane next week, and I will get you at the airport," she insisted.

After I had prayed about it, I felt that I should go, so I went home, arranged for the girls to stay with two of my sisters — two with each one — did my laundry, and caught the plane to Ashland. Ruth met me as she had promised.

When I stepped onto the Calvary Pentecostal Campground and experienced for the first time the victorious praise and worship that is the hallmark of that place, I felt like leaping and never stopping. I felt a kinship with the people of the camp, who were obviously giving their all for God in such freedom, living in community, ready and willing to be sent at any moment to any nation in the world at the voice of the Lord.

I met Rev. Wallace Heflin, Sr. and his wife, Edith, wonderful saints who were Ruth's parents and pastors of the work, and I met her brother, Rev. Wallace Heflin, Jr.

The prophetic stream in the camp was glorious, and God repeated to me during those first days many things that He had told me in secret through the years.

That week a distinguished visitor arrived at the campground, Rev. Arthur Dodzweit, called by those who knew him well, The Father of African Missions. My husband and I had known him for many years. He was one of the Elim group of missionaries and was a man loved by many thousands of people in the African continent where he had served for many years. He was truly an end-time apostle, a man greatly loved of God and a man of great love. I was surprised to see him because I didn't know that he knew the Heflin family. He was equally surprised to see me. He had not heard that my husband had died and was wondering what I was doing so far from home.

Rev. Dodzweit preached that afternoon, and when he had given the altar call, the power of God fell in that place. For a long time we lingered in the rosy glow of the glory of God, and I felt my life taking a new turn. When nearly everyone else had gone, Brother Dodzweit beckoned me to come forward and began to prophesy over me. Through him God told me that I was to stay at the camp and live and minister there and other wondrous things about the future.

That night a strange thing began. When the evening meetings were over, I would retire and fall asleep. Then, about 2 a.m. each night, the Lord would wake me up by coming to my bedside. The first night He said to me, "Do not leave this place. Stay here fast by my maidens. My daughter, do not leave this place." I began to weep and yield, weep and yield. On another night the Lord said to me over and over, "My daughter, do not leave this place. I want you to be here when I come for My Church." It was an awesome and slightly frightening experience in which I came to understand why the Lord had said so many times in Scripture to those with whom He was dealing, *"Fear not."*

To Zacharias:

*But the angel said unto him, FEAR NOT, Zach-
arias: for thy prayer is heard; and thy wife Elisabeth
shall bear thee a son, and thou shalt call his name
John.* Luke 1:13

To Mary:

*And the angel said unto her, FEAR NOT, Mary: for
thou hast found favour with God.* Luke 1:30

To Joseph:

*But while he thought on these things, behold, the
angel of the Lord appeared unto him in a dream,
saying, Joseph, thou son of David, FEAR NOT to
take unto thee Mary thy wife: for that which is con-
ceived in her is of the Holy Ghost.* Matthew 1:20

To the shepherds:

*And the angel said unto them, FEAR NOT: for, be-
hold, I bring you good tidings of great joy, which
shall be to all people.* Luke 2:10

To Simon Peter:

*And so was also James, and John, the sons of
Zebedee, which were partners with Simon. And
Jesus said unto Simon, FEAR NOT; from hence-
forth thou shalt catch men.* Luke 5:10

To the women at the tomb:

And the angel answered and said unto the women,

*FEAR NOT ye: for I know that ye seek Jesus, which
was crucified.*   Matthew 28:5

I was experiencing the fear of a new thing and, at the
same time I was experiencing a great breaking within.
God had to do some spring plowing in me before He
could plant a new seed with its potential for new life. The
fallow ground had to be broken up. The next week I flew
back to Philadelphia, collected my four daughters and
some clothes for the five of us and, together, we drove
back to Virginia.

In the coming days, when I would drive into town to
get something, I could sense the Lord saying, "Yield."
When I came upon a traffic sign saying YIELD, sometimes I put my head down on the steering wheel and
wept because I was being broken for the new thing that
God was about to do in me.

Brother Dodzweit saw me weeping in the services and
his eyes filled with tears as well. "I know what's happening to you," he assured me. As I thought about it, it
seemed that he was sent by God as an emissary from the
Elim group to ensure that I was spiritually well taken
care of and settled into a new place. He hadn't even
known that I was there, but God knew and sent him to
smooth the way for me into the new life before me.

During that summer we experienced some unique visitations from the Lord in the Ladies' Dormitory where the
girls and I were staying. One night a woman was led back
to the dorm, completely under the power of the Spirit. As
we put her to bed, I felt the air vibrating around us. "Turn
the lights out," I said to the others, "God is going to do
something special."

The lights were turned out, but the atmosphere continued to vibrate, and soon we were visited by hundreds of

angels. Some only felt their presence, but many of us saw them. You can imagine our excitement. The air was filled with the shouts of our praise and with speaking in tongues. One sister cried out in joy as she described angels two stories high. Another saw the ceiling full of cherubs' faces, singing.

The angels took the young missionary girls and rolled them from the arms of one angel to the arms of another. Some were rolling on the beds and others on the floor. Women who had never prophesied in their lives began to prophesy. In general, there was a trembling and a visitation that lasted for an hour and a half in the pitch dark — a visitation that we shall never forget.

God made Himself real in so many ways during that first campmeeting. One night He told me, "I have given you as a gift to this campground, and I want you to stay here and pour into the people everything that I have taught you." By the time camp was over that year, I knew that I would be a permanent part of that place. The Heflin family accepted us gladly, knowing that God had led us there.

The Lord told me to sell my house in Pennsylvania. In a vision He showed me the sign of a realtor that I had known about but whom I had never used. In the vision the sign showed the sale price crossed out and marked SOLD. So I knew exactly who to call. I called him and told him that I wanted to sell the property. In a tight money market, the house was sold in two days, and I prepared to travel to Pennsylvania to sign the papers.

My moving to a Pentecostal campground aroused resentment and suspicion on the part of some family members. They had no understanding of a real experience with the Lord or that one's life plan is to be determined by Him and not ourselves. There was concern that I was doing foolish things with my money. Their inquiries grew more angry every day, and family lawyers were consulted.

I was told by God in prophecy, "I have brought you here to keep you safe, " and now the Lord told me to go up to Philadelphia only when He indicated. One day the Lord told me to go up on the plane in the morning and to come home in the afternoon. My sister is a Christian and she stood with me through those difficult days. She was there the day of the settlement. I had her, my lawyer, and the real estate agent all together at the same table and settled the affairs of my former life in one day.

When I felt that I had to go right back the same day, she was wonderful about it. She packed all of our belongings later and shipped them to us. When they arrived, they were put into storage because we had no place to keep them at the moment.

Everything God told me to do, I consulted with my pastors. Most of us who lived through the 60s in the Charismatic movement remember those who began to feel totally free from the restraint of submitting to any pastor. They determined never to sign on the dotted line of church membership, but I never felt that way myself. God always told me to put myself under the dominion of the best, Holy-Ghost-power-filled, fasting-and-praying, joyful, Bible-preaching, tongues-talking-and-dancing pastor in town and do what he said, and be there when the door was open and fast and pray and carry on. So I said to the Heflin family, "Do you have such a thing as church membership?"

"Yes," they replied. "It's called opening the church door."

"Well, open the door," I said, "Here I come. God told me not to leave, so I'd better sign my name on the dotted line." I believe that if God puts you in a place you must stand there for Him.

I had gotten a prophecy that said: "God is going to make you a pillar here."

I said, "Lord, your pillar is going to stand here and bear some weight now. Just load it on me."

Not long afterward, Sister Edith Heflin told me that God had revealed to her that I should be the new treasurer of the church and camp ministry. At this news, all my children hooted because I had never, despite all my learning and love of reading and years of study in college, excelled at math. In fact, my dislike for the subject was one thread that always ran through my life, like the love of Jesus. I didn't like mathematics or bookkeeping of any type. Why was the Lord choosing me for this position? Once again I trusted Him for new orders.

From the moment I heard the pastor's words, I said *Amen*; then I went home to my room and fell before the Lord and cried out, "Lord Jesus, help me." In that moment, I felt a tremendous pressure and weight of His presence, and He spoke to me and said, "Now, arise and open My Word." I cracked the Bible open and read the words before me:

> *And Shabbethai and Jozabad, of the chiefs of the Levites, had the oversight of the outward business of the house of God.*   Nehemiah 11:16

What could I say? I cried, "AMEN, Lord. There is an anointing that goes with this position. Let me have it now." I quickly settled into the position He had given me, and these many years I have joyfully performed the service — because it was initiated by His voice.

I had my own finances to think of too. As a widow, I

had been left very well-off. I kept most of the money invested and had a small amount coming in each month for our necessities. It seemed like the Lord's provision for the early years of my travels, as I was adjusting to the life of faith. However, I didn't feel rich. I felt like a keeper of God's money. I had an obligation to listen carefully to His voice in my giving.

That first summer was wonderful in this regard. Someone would receive a prophecy that they were to go to South America, and I would joyfully write out a check for the amount they needed (the information having been discreetly obtained from one of the pastors). When there was an appeal for new buildings, it pleased me to make an inquiry as to the total cost involved, and what joy it gave me to underwrite the project. I was beginning to enter into the joy of giving, giving by faith, giving as I heard God speak. This, I found, is the test of giving, whether you have much money or not.

Personally, I think it is harder to give when you have more. It requires that you turn off your mind and tune in to what the Spirit is saying, because the mind always has other, conflicting thoughts. We must come to the place with our money that we pray, like Jesus:

> *Nevertheless not my will, but Thine, be done.*
> Luke 22:42

It is true what the Lord has said:

> *For where your treasure is, there will your heart be also.*   Matthew 6:21

I learned that summer not to lay up treasures for myself. I could have claimed that as a legitimate concern. After all, I was a widow and had no other source of income, but God wanted me to trust Him. I learned not to worry about the future because it was in God's hands. The One who asked of me some financial expenditure one day was well able to take care of me on the next.

As time progressed, I gave anonymously winter coats, dental work and plane tickets. When there was a call of God to have a meeting in a certain place, it was my great joy to find out the cost of the rental of the auditorium and pay it — all of this known only to the pastors. That is the type of giving I believe in, hearing the voice of God and quietly obeying.

As I learned to give joyfully, I lost all fear for the future. I knew Who held tomorrow, and I knew that He was holding my hand. Little did I know that He would provide for my needs in a worldwide ministry.

Chapter 5

Out To the Nations

Therefore will I give thanks unto thee, O Lord, among the heathen, and sing praises unto thy name.
Psalm 18:49

One of the highlights of that first glorious summer was an altar call for those who had a burden for the release of the Jews of Russia. That nation, feared by much of the world for so long, had recently opened for tourism, and the Spirit was bidding us to go forth and prophesy the release of the Jewish people who were restricted and/or imprisoned there.

As the first northern woman to come to live at the campground, I had some advantage in this regard. For much of my young life, I had been raised near Jewish people. Grandfather lived in a large home in a beautiful neighborhood where many Jews lived, and he also had many of them as business friends. When mother remarried, we moved into a neighborhood that was very handsome, with many large homes, and many of my new schoolmates were Jewish. I grew to love them as a people.

When I was only twelve and the Second World War came to an end, I remember watching a newsreel in a public place that showed the tragic pile of starved bodies in the concentration camps of Auswitz and Bergen Belsen. I could see the horror and sadness on the faces of the American officers as they marched into the camps and witnessed the grizzly sight for the first time. I witnessed their determination to display the bodies for all the world to see what a monster Hitler had been. I saw them providing the dead with a decent burial, mass graves attended to by military bulldozers. As I watched, horrified, I sprang to my feet in that public place and cried out with tears, "Lord Jesus, let me help them."

When I was in my late teens, television announced the proclamation of the State of Israel (we had just acquired our first television set). When I saw the blue and white Mogen David, the star of David on the Jewish flag, unfurled for the first time, I wept.

Yes, I loved the Jewish people. Yes, I would respond to the Spirit's wooing to go forth and work for their release from Russia. I went to the altar. I have always thought it was wonderful that many southern Pentecostal people, who had not been raised around Jewish people as I had, rose to their feet and responded to the Spirit's call as well. About fifty of us wept before the altar that afternoon. Very few of the group had any money, but within a few weeks we were boarding an aircraft that would take us to Moscow and to Jerusalem. God had provided all the necessary tickets.

I took two of my daughters along to Russia that year. It took a great deal of money, but I did not hesitate to take them. My late husband and I had always tried to do what was best for them, enrolling all of them in a Christian school. Since there were four of them spread out over a very few years, that was costly. At one point, we had to sell our house and buy a less expensive one and move closer to one of the best Christian schools. We could not afford to leave a single stone unturned. We did not want to blame ourselves in future years and wonder what we should have done. Whatever the cost, I would do what was best for them now.

Regarding my children, the Lord often told me, "You shall not pass this way again. What I tell you to do for them you must do now." That included Russia and Israel. When Abraham was told to do something by the Lord, he *"commanded his children after him."*

Russia was my first overseas mission. Some have thought that to do a mission overseas you must go somewhere and establish a church or establish a Bible school; but the Word of God is powerful to accomplish its purpose. What we were doing was very biblical, going to a country, not to stay, not to teach, perhaps not even to preach (in places where it was forbidden by law), but to prophesy over the people, over the countryside, over the political system, and over the Kremlin, to pray and cry out to God in our hotel rooms at night. As we did this, I knew that someday we would see a modern-day exodus of the Jews from Russia. It took many years, but God did indeed fulfill His word.

The next great trip the Spirit of God outlined for our camp people was a three-month evangelistic effort the following spring on the streets of London, England. When the Lord began to speak to us about taking a team of missionaries there, I was not immediately inclined to join the mission. I had no problem with the concept of personal evangelism. I had been a soul-winner for many years already. I have never understood how anyone can know that there is a Heaven and a Hell and not seek to turn people away from the latter. This is the reason we are here, and God has no other plan than to use our voices to preach His Word.

My reticence was not because of the mission, but because of the destination. England was not one of my favorite places, harking back to some very painful teenage memories of having an alcoholic English stepfather. As I stood in the altar one day, thinking that what God was saying was for everyone else but me, I suddenly had a vision of the Twin Towers of London, and I knew that my name was on the ticket. I made provision for my daughters to be cared for by some of the missionaries who were staying behind, and I joined the team.

There were thirty of us, of all ages, fifteen men and fifteen ladies. We rented a house in Clapham Pond, a suburb of London (the girls lived on one floor and the men on another), and prepared our own meals in the morning and evening. We came together to pray several times a day. As we prayed during those first days, the Holy Ghost outlined our mission in London. We were to go out by twos, two men together or two ladies together, traveling about by double-decker buses (we each purchased a bus ticket for unlimited travel), to go where God had shown us in prayer on the city map and to witness to people everywhere. Some of us stood by the marble arch in Hyde Park where all the preachers stand. Some stood in Victoria Station, while others preached in Trafalgar Square.

London has the reputation of being a sophisticated and unyielding city, but we were believing God to bring revival. The task set for us by the Holy Ghost was a great one, for some Londoners were offended by our efforts. They had no desire to hear more about God or to reveal their feelings about religious things. "Go home, Yankees," they called out. "Oh, here is Billy Graham," they heckled. I had been a Bible teacher since I was sixteen in the Episcopalian Church, but this was something new for me, a whole race of "private" people. What intensive training!

Not all the reactions were negative. Some shouted, "Good work!" and other encouraging phrases, as they passed by. One man who was overjoyed by our presence was himself a witness for Christ and went about carrying a sandwich board with Scriptures on the front and back and placards in his hand. Tears filled his eyes as he saw us preaching in Trafalgar Square during the final three-day crusade. He shouted out to the people around him, "See, you told me I was crazy, and now these people are coming to tell you the very same thing. Jesus is coming again. Are they crazy too?" Some onlookers thought that man was indeed unbalanced, but he wasn't. The most balanced man in the crowd is the one who tells others that Jesus is coming soon.

During those final days, each of us had an opportunity to speak to the crowd of Londoners who gathered. Some of those who spoke were very eloquent. I, however, was not accustomed to speaking before such a crowd and was concerned about how I would conduct myself on such a public platform. My turn came after I had been standing for many hours on my feet while others took their turn. When they handed me the microphone, I was not sure what I would say or do. Suddenly, something happened that helped me immensely: A drunken heckler appeared, twirling around and making fun of our dancing in the Spirit and praising God. I was so angry at the devil who would try to mock God and teach others to mock God that I started to preach like a house on fire. It seemed as if liquid lava was coming out of me. All the butterflies were gone from my stomach. At the end, one of the leaders said to me, "We didn't know you had that much fire in you." That was the beginning of a whole lot of fire for God, and I have never had a fear of public speaking since that day

The devil had done his utmost to rob me of that day of victory. Back at the campground in Ashland, I passed the winter with the girls in a tiny cabin by the camp road, with scarcely any heat and sometimes no water. It was wonderful! It was the provision of the Lord for the moment and a test of our faith and faithfulness.

Early one morning, as I was going to the outhouse in the semidarkness, I tripped over a strand of barbed wire is a fence that kept the ponies in their pasture. I didn't realize then how badly I was injured, but after several days my leg began to swell horribly. Although there was no opening in the leg, I had apparently bruised the bone, and an infection resulted. I was determined not to go to a doctor, but to allow the Lord to heal me, and everyone prayed for me in the meetings. Still, that leg continued to be inflamed and eventually grew to three times its natural size.

The devil said to me one night, "You have blood poisoning." I told him emphatically that it was nothing that Jesus couldn't handle and refused to speak with him any more on the subject. Several nights later the pain was so intense that I could not go to the service. Pastor Heflin, Sr. sent for me and asked me to come to the altar. As I laid at the altar and cried out to God, I saw a vision of a tiny squirt of water leave my leg. At that moment one of the sisters came over to me and said, "There's a doctor from India here. I believe that God would have him to lance your leg and get out the infection." I agreed. Several people held my hands and prayed for me as the doctor took a sterile razor and opened a two inch incision in my leg. Sure enough, out came about a pint of infection and blood.

I didn't want any stitches. I was sure that if they would just put some gauze over the wound, with a little olive oil to keep my stocking from sticking, I would be fine. It was several months before the wound healed entirely, and it was during that time that the Lord spoke to me to go on the London trip. I was determined to obey Him, although some people warned me against traveling with my injury. As I stood that last night in our church in Callao, Virginia, I saw a vision (with my eyes open). I saw Jesus standing in a bright road ahead of me. There were angels with large, white wings and flowing white robes walking behind Him on each side. He turned to me and looked with such love and confidence and pride and said to me, "Your faith is well-spoken-of in the heavenlies." I knew then that I could go to the mission field with my leg still open, and that nothing adverse would happen to me.

While we were in England, the Lord told me to soak my leg in a clean, white plastic vessel at night in very hot water and a little handful of salt. Within ten days, the wound had closed up entirely and I was, at last, healed.

We returned home with many victories. That was the first of several successful campaigns in England.

When we got back from that trip, I began to build a house. When we moved to the camp, I hadn't known if I would ever have another house, but the Lord began to tell me, before that first summer was over, "Build! Build! Build!" I would have been perfectly satisfied to lived in one of the community cabins with the girls, and I have maintained that attitude since then. You can be so content in the will of God that it doesn't matter what you have been accustomed to. I am perfectly happy where He wants me. For His sake, I can come out of a mansion and live in a hut. When you have that settled, you have taken care of many of the issues of life.

The Lord had said, "Build! Build! Build!" but I was unsure of what exactly I should build. My personal feeling was to build something small. Talking to my pastors clarified my goal. They said, "Don't build a tiny cabin. Build something nice. You will need it some day." Brother Heflin Senior then went out and staked out an area on his own land showing where he would like the house to sit and which way he would like it to face.

I prayed for God's guidance and drew up the plans He showed me, and the building started. We started, not with a well-known contractor, but with some of the preachers and missionaries at the campground: Rev. Willie Vaughan, a master carpenter and preacher, who built many buildings on the campground, was the overseer of the work. Rev. Wallace Heflin, Jr., the pastor's son, and Jay Rawlings from Canada helped. Brother Lester Daughtridge from North Carolina did the brick work. And many others contributed as well.

Using volunteer labor, the house took a long time to build. Often, when we were running for materials, Brother Heflin Senior would say to me, "This house would have driven anyone else into a nervous breakdown."

I answered, "Well, that's simply not possible when you heard about it from the Lord."

The work was finally completed, and the house turned out beautifully. We had a house warming, during which the Lord spoke to us by prophecy and said: *My presence shall dwell like a thick cloud in this place.*

Brother Heflin Senior was the last to leave that day. It is one of the things I fondly remember about him since he went to be with the Lord in 1972. He looked at me and smiled and, with an anointed shine on his face, said, "There's a good spirit in this house." That night I gathered my girls in my arms, looked up to Jesus and together we thanked God for His faithfulness. He had taken away our former life, but He had brought us safely and abundantly into a new and better one, a life of faith and fruitfulness.

When God sets you in a place, you are well established.

I thank Him for His abundant provision for our lives. He is truly Jehovah Jirah. He is able to see what we need, not only for the moment but also for the future. That is the great difference between us and God. He sees what lies down the road far beyond our line of sight. He knows what He requires of us and what we will be doing in days to come, and He provides for every step of the way, in the *then* and in the *now*.

Oh, how precious and lovely He is!

Chapter 6

Brazil

As soon as they hear of me, they shall obey me: the strangers shall submit themselves unto me.

Psalm 18:44

During the second summer season I was at the campground God began to do a marvelous thing in South America. A few months before He had given us the use of a beautiful, well-built, modern campground situated high in the Andes Mountains, outside of Quito, the capital city of Ecuador, and great revival had broken out there. Each area of the world seems to have its particular time for visitation from God, and it was now South America's time.

I had a special interest in South America because years ago my grandfather's half-brother, Charles Kennedy, one of the boys who had been raised to be an ice cream manufacturer by my great-grandfather, had been asked to go to South America by an Argentine businessman. Together, he and my uncle Charles, later fondly called *Carlos* by his

Argentine countrymen, had started the first ice cream company in that country.

There in Argentina, Uncle Charles accepted the Lord Jesus Christ, and among the young ladies living in a British colony there he found a girl named Alice Lowe, the daughter of New Zealand missionaries, and he married her. Through the years Uncle Carlos became an elder in the Brethren Church, a large home-owner and the father of six children — five girls and one boy, all about my age. This family had been used by God to witness to my life about the Lord Jesus Christ when I was still very young. It was Charles' sister, Catherine, who was the *Aunt Catherine* who had meant so much to me when I was a child. It was she who had overseen my decision for Christ. She had encouraged me, given me my first Bible, taken me to her home for vacations, and prayed with me.

Uncle Charles had visited grandfather through the years, and his oldest daughter, my cousin Joanna (who was exactly my age), had come to live one year with my grandmother when I was also living with her. So we were close. After she returned to Argentina, we corresponded. The fact that she wrote to me half in English and half in Spanish forced me to learn a little of that language so that I could understand the letters. I was very excited, therefore, when it seemed that an evangelistic trip was being planned for South America, a trip which would include the exciting new campground in Ecuador and also include a stop in Argentina. I was thrilled with the thought of seeing Uncle Carlos and Aunt Alice again and of meeting the rest of the family. The tour was also to include Brazil.

As the time approached and I was praying and seeking the Lord one night in my house, I felt the entire room filled with His presence. The children were asleep and I was alone. I had told the Lord that I didn't want to sleep that night, that I wanted to seek Him instead and that I expected some special spiritual birthday gift from my heavenly Father.

As I began to pray, the darkened room lit up and before me stood my precious Savior, in such power that my eyes turned immediately into a fountain of tears. I was so weak in His awesome presence that I could do nothing but fall over under that power on the sofa; and I couldn't get up. He stood before me and spoke clearly, "Go to Brazil. Go to Ouro Preto, Minas Gerais and Belo Horizonte." Although I had probably seen these cities on a map at sometime, I had never thought of going to any of them before.

I said, *YES*, as usual, *YES* to everything this strange appearance signified. After a time, God's presence quietly subsided in the room. To show Him my sincerity, I went into the bedroom, took out a suitcase and put something into it.

In the church meetings that followed, several people prophesied over me, one by one, and said, "I see you under a glory cloud. God is giving you a whole nation." I was afraid to tell anyone what God had told me in private; for I had seen myself alone, not with the entire group. I was not yet an accomplished preacher. Except for that brief experience in London and the short messages I gave sometimes at the young people's service in church, I had not preached over a microphone. I was confident, however, that what God calls you *to* He equips you *for* and even causes you to excel in. On the other hand, I didn't know what God wanted of me, and I was a bit fearful. I didn't know whether any of the greatly used preachers in my new home would even think I was worthy of going out alone, so I began to make plans to go on the tour with everyone else.

Originally, the plan was to go to Brazil and Argentina, and then finish up at Quito, but as the weeks wore on, the Holy Spirit told Brother Heflin, Jr. to go the opposite way: Quito first, Argentina, and then Brazil. I was sure the change was just for me because I sensed that I would be staying on beyond the limited time of the tour.

I acquired a good baby-sitter from among the missionaries to live in my house with the girls while I was gone, and I bought my ticket for the trip to South America. Two weeks before we left, I had gone to bed one night when something strange happened. I was amazed to feel the atmosphere of the room pulsate and vibrate with excitement, just as it had done that night the angels had visited the ladies dormitory the year before. The presence of Jesus, when He comes, is all consuming and overpowering and grips your entire thought and soul in His presence; but this was different. I threw myself on my knees, thinking that I was about to have a visitation from Heaven; and I was not disappointed. I looked up, and there, standing by the foot of my bed, were two angels. They were about five or five and a half feet tall and of classically beautiful face and form. They looked like transparent wax. They had beautiful expressions on their faces and were entirely friendly and loving.

They did not speak out loud, but I understood when one looked at the other and said, without audible words, "We are angels, but she is one of the redeemed." That one sentence showed me that there is a communication in the Spirit in Heaven of which we know nothing. It needs no sound. It is truly *in the Spirit*. It also told me that the angels respect our position as beings who are redeemed by the blood of Jesus Christ, something they cannot fully understand, but which they respect, nevertheless.

One angel looked at me and pointed his finger at me. He was so loving and respectful as he said, "They shall call you *The Angel of the Amazon*." I understood then that I was receiving instruction directly from Heaven and that the Amazon region of Brazil would be part of my itinerary.

Two weeks later we embarked on our journey. Arriving in Quito, we were thrilled to see the beauty of the place that the Lord had built for revival. It was so well done. Some of the cabins were A-frame chalet-type buildings. The gardens were lovely and well kept; and the entire camp was set against the backdrop of Mount Cotopaxi, the highest active volcano in the world (yet perpetually snow-capped). Our friends, Rev. Harold McDougal and his wife Diane were in charge of the place.

The spiritual atmosphere in the crusade in Quito was just as lovely. The people were hungry; wonderful choruses of revival were being sung; and our efforts were backed up by the life of fasting and prayer and Bible study of the missionaries and students in that place. I will never forget it. Many people came to worship and stayed to be taught. There was a wonderful sense of unity in the place, and a great work was done for God.

To this point I had not dared to tell Brother Heflin that I was planning to stay in Brazil. Right or wrong that was the first time I had withheld something from my pastors. The appearance of God made me to understand that I could not disobey Him. I had to go. That, however, was counterbalanced by the fear that my spiritual leaders would not think I was ready for such a mission alone. How little I understood, in those early days, of their willingness, even eagerness, to see others go and be used of God!

Toward the end of the Quito meetings, I took Brother

Heflin and Brother McDougal aside and told them what God had shown me. At first they were surprised, but then, as usual, their great reliance on the Lord led them to say, "Let us pray for you." As they prayed, prophecy came forth in which the Lord truly confirmed to them and to the company that this was indeed His will.

Those messages were later written down, and I carried them with me for many years. I still have them and record them here:

Quito, Ecuador
November 18, 1973

The Lord would say unto thee:

> *Rest in the Lord. It is not needful that thou shouldest try to force anything in thyself. For if the Lord say this, do it; if He say that, do it; if He say nothing at all, then just keep content in the will and praising of the Lord.*

> *For the Lord's ways are so high, wonderful and great. Sometimes He speaks them piece by piece. He does not always reveal the whole purpose in one moment. But even as a first step is taken, God shall reveal Himself; and as the next step is taken, God shall reveal Himself; and as the next step is taken, God shall reveal Himself.*

> *At times, it would seem to thee thou art doing nothing at all. Thou wouldst be tempted to think that thou hast not accomplished the thing that God has said; but a word at a time, and a step at a time, faith in God for the moment, trust in the Lord at the moment. Hast thou not experienced in the days that are gone that this has often been the way?*

And the Lord would say to thee:

> *Do not worry. Do not fret. Just say, "Here I am,*
> *Lord! Do with me as Thou dost desire. Work out*
> *every detail of Thy purposes, and help me not to fail*
> *Thee in any way."*

> *If thy heart is thus right in the sight of the Lord,*
> *shall He not say further unto thee:*

> *As thou dost march along, the purposes of the Lord*
> *shall be revealed and unfolded and thou shalt be able*
> *to say in thine heart, "Thank You, Jesus. This is*
> *what Thou hast desired of me."*

And the Lord would speak further unto thee and, yea, He would say:

> *The first step, my daughter, is a step of good-byes;*
> *for thou shalt say good-bye to this one, and thou*
> *shalt say good-bye to that one, and thou shalt say*
> *good-bye to this, and thou shalt say good-bye to that,*
> *and thou shalt say, "But, Lord, I am so alone."*

> *And thou shalt say hello to thy Lord in a new way,*
> *for He hath a mighty thing for thee; yea, He hath a*
> *great work. Receive ye the strength of thy God; for*
> *thy mouth shall be exalted in warning, and thou*
> *shalt lead many to safety. Close thyself in with thy*
> *God; for He hath much for thee; for He loveth thee.*
> *He yearneth over thee. Yea, close thyself in.*

Thus saith the Lord.

Before we boarded the airplane in Quito, Brother Heflin looked at me; then, turning to look at the safety and security of the brethren who were carrying on the work in Quito and thinking perhaps that this was the place I should stay, asked, "Are you sure this is not the place you should stay?"

"I am sure," I answered confidently. So, on we flew to Buenos Aires, Argentina.

After we had arrived and were settled into our hotel, Uncle Carlos met us and took us to Maximo Paz, the Word of Life Youth Camp, located in the plains outside of Buenos Aires. The camp was run by his son, William (my cousin). It was November, and there were no meetings in progress, but the staff of the camp received us with the traditional *mate* drink, a hot tea served in an Indian gourd with beautifully embellished silver chasings on it. We sipped the pungent tea through *bombillas*, copper or brass tubes, very much like straws.

What a joy it was to see my pastor walking about with Uncle Carlos and Cousin William, camp leaders for Jesus in opposite hemispheres, as they showed us the Argentine camp! We had a lot in common with them, and conversation covered everything from sleeping capacity and expected participation during the next camp season to proposed camp expansion for the future. They showed us their new buildings and the pool that was under construction. We had a wonderful time of fellowship and praise and worship together.

Other members of the family came too. My cousin Florence, with whom I had also corresponded as a child, was now a medical doctor. She came down, with her husband, from their estate in the hills — where they had a *mate* plantation and a clinic where she practiced her profession. Aunt Alice, who was still very active and who worked with her husband distributing Scripture portions up and down the length of the country, was there, too.

They took me to preach at a girl's school where my cousin, Betty, is a teacher. (Incidentally, Betty had been the translator for Brother Heflin on his previous visit with two other young men to hold meetings in Argentine churches.)

When we were about to leave this comfortable Christian enclave, and my dear family was looking at me longingly, wishing I could stay there, Brother Heflin again asked me the question: "Are you sure this is not the place you are to stay?"

I said, "No, this is not the place," and we departed.

As we flew over the border from Argentina into Brazil, the Lord spoke to me to read Psalm 18, the words God had always given me when He was about to change direction in my life.

As I read it this time, I had a visitation of the Spirit of God there in my airplane seat. Deep breaking and sobbing came in my soul, and tears ran from my eyes like a fountain as my eyes fell upon the words:

> *For thou wilt light my candle: the Lord my God will enlighten my darkness.*
> *For by thee I have run through a troop; and by my God have I leaped over a wall.*
> *As for God, his way is perfect: the word of the Lord is tried: he is a buckler to all those that trust in him.*
> *For who is God save the Lord? or who is a rock save our God?*
> *It is God that girdeth me with strength, and maketh my way perfect.*
> *He maketh my feet like hinds' feet, and setteth me upon my high places.*

> *He teacheth my hands to war, so that a bow of steel is
> broken by mine arms.*
> *Thou hast also given me the shield of thy salvation:
> and thy right hand hath holden me up, and thy
> gentleness hath made me great.*
> *Thou hast enlarged my steps under me, that my feet
> did not slip.*   Psalm 18:28-36

The next verses I read contain the great missionary protective utterance:

> *Thou hast delivered me from the strivings of the
> people; and thou hast made me the head of the hea-
> then: a people whom I have not known shall serve
> me.*
> *As soon as they hear of me, they shall obey me: the
> strangers shall submit themselves unto me.*
>   Psalm 18:43-44

Oh, glory to the Living God! That word lit up my soul,
and I felt the whole armor of the Holy Ghost being placed
on me for the battle ahead. Again I heard the Lord's
voice, saying: "Go into Brazil, nothing doubting."

When we arrived in Rio de Janeiro, the entire team was
invited to the platform of the great Assembly of God
Church in Sao Cristavao. The great missionary pastor
and leader of his people, then and now, Tulio Barros, was
in the pulpit. For eighty-one years the movement of holiness, power and evangelism had manifest itself in the
Assemblies of God of Brazil. These brethren had stood
for the Word and had increased to eight million members.

After a series of wonderful meetings in the church, and
of experiencing the wonderful hospitality of the church,
Brother Heflin stood and dropped his bombshell: "God

has spoken to Sister Viola Weidemann to stay in Brazil for a time." (He had consulted with Brother Tulio before making this announcement.) Thus, he committed me, a widow, into the hands of the leadership of the Assemblies of God of Brazil. Because the Brazilian Assemblies had been under the old Swedish school of missions, they had not permitted women to preach. My translator later told me that I was the first woman to do so. All the glory belongs to God!

A ripple of surprise went through the audience when Brother Heflin made that announcement, surprise that God would visit them with an American woman to be a preacher in their midst. As the announcement was made, one of the old prophets of the congregation stood up (perhaps even against his own will), and the Spirit of God thundered through him in a word with such force that his glasses continually threatened to fall from his face as he spoke. He could barely stand as the message came forth, a message to me from God, before them all:

My servant, I have given you a great net; I have made you a fisher of men; and I will give you great victory.

I was content. The Word of the Lord would be satisfied.

As I saw the members of the team off that week, each of them happy about a campaign well done for the Lord in Brazil, about a fruitful trip to South America, and about the prospect of returning home, Brother Heflin turned to me and playfully dangled the homeward portion of my airline ticket (which I could no longer use and would lose) before me. Smiling, he said, "Do you want to change your mind?"

"I can't," I replied, as the tears ran uncontrollably

down my face. I stood with my host and the translator, Brother Nataniel Betenmiller, and my hostess, Arita Pessoa, from Sao Cristavao, the wife of the treasurer of the church, and waved a bittersweet farewell to my people. The Lord had not told me how long to stay, but I sensed in that moment that I would be staying far longer than I had anticipated.

I stayed with the Pessoa family in their beautiful marble mansion, and every day Brother Betenmiller would come, either with his wife or with a son or daughter (he had ten children) and take me to the arranged meetings. For what turned out to be the next three and a half months of exciting revival in Brazil, he laid down his own life and picked up the will of the Lord.

He was, without a doubt, chosen of God for this task. He had been a faithful pastor of the Assemblies of God for more than thirty years. He was also so deeply respected both for his intellect and his spiritual character that he worked in the church's publishing house. He knew virtually every pastor of their group, both in the large cities and in every way station in the nation. As time went on, I found that he loved to preach on the streets, loved to go out carrying the Gospel, loved people and was everyone's pastor. He was, indeed, an ideal ministerial companion for my journeys.

We began locally, and from the moment I took the microphone for the first time, in Rio and in Sao Cristavao, great grace was given to me. I never lacked a message, having asked the Lord every step of the way what He wanted to say to the people. I was amazed how simple it is to know what the message of the Lord is for each place.

Every time I stood in the pulpit I felt God's mighty presence and power and knew that I had the message for the people. I was amazed by the variety of messages that God gave me, but then He knows the need of men's hearts.

There were afternoon meetings in which the crowds were as small as seven hundred (seven hundred is small to the Brazilian Assemblies of God). The crowds at the night meetings were larger, usually counted in the thousands rather than the hundreds. There were many miracles of healing in these meetings and, in each of those meetings, from forty-five to eighty people were filled with the Holy Ghost.

I will never forget one memorable case of healing in a large church. A woman approached me holding her head and said that she suffered from migraine headaches. I began to prophesy over her. The Spirit said to her, "I want you to worship me, and I want you to stop talking about other people. When you stop talking about other people, the headaches will stop." She wept and repented, and the headaches stopped and never returned. Some of the people of the church got a valuable lesson by hearing that word of prophecy, all of them nodding to the truth of the fact of what God was saying. Praise the Lord!

If I had not been told that these pastors did not welcome women ministers, I would never have known it. They were extremely cordial and cooperative, for the most part. When we were finished in a town, sometimes the pastors or deacons would take us halfway to the next, meeting the pastors of the next town. On other occasions, we went by bus. Always a warm welcome awaited us. "How do you explain it?" Brother Betenmiller asked. These people didn't like Americans; they didn't like women preachers; and they didn't like missionaries; but they love you."

"That's simple," I told him, "these people love God and want revival, however it comes."

I went to a meeting the next day feeling quiet and drained of strength. As I leaned on the pulpit before I preached, an old blind man groped his way up the aisle and came to me. I put out my hand gently on his head, and his eyes were opened instantly. The whole church rejoiced.

During the weeks and months that followed, there was never any lack of activity. We were pulled in every direction by the needs of the people who had heard about the miracles that God was doing. They came to get me one morning toward the end of November to minister in a prayer meeting. We were told that a young man who had once known the Lord had fallen into sin and was now completely possessed with demons and needed deliverance. When we arrived at the meeting, we found them singing a slow hymn to try to free him. I had stepped into a new place in God where I found myself thinking His thoughts, and I knew by the Spirit what had to be done. I stopped all activity and asked the man's name.

"His name is Luis," I was told.

"Luis," I said, in a commanding voice, "stand up, in the name of Jesus Christ."

At first, Luis didn't move. Then, very suddenly, his body flipped over in a supernatural feat of Satan that no athlete could have duplicated. His eyes rolled back in his head, and his hands were formed into claws. God said to me, "Speak to the man. His own spirit got him into this, and his own spirit will get him out. It is his decision."

I have found that every case is different and that the Lord does not have a blanket answer for every situation, so I obeyed, commanding him again, as the Spirit bade me: "Luis, stand up, in the name of Jesus Christ." With that, he staggered to his feet like a drunken man. "Luis," I said, "you have sinned and gotten yourself into this. Confess all your sin." He did so, with tears.

As Luis began to weep and confess his sin before the Lord, he received salvation. Within a few moments I laid my hands on him, and he was filled with the Holy Ghost. I later found that many of the church leaders had opposed praying for backsliders to be filled with the Spirit so quickly. They felt that a returning backslider had to be weighed and examined for at least six months to see if he was worthy even of being rebaptized in water, let alone receive the Holy Ghost.

"This man has been delivered from satanic oppression," I told them. "The Holy Spirit coming into him now is the only thing that will strengthen him and protect him against Satan's power in the future," and they seemed satisfied.

The Lord said to me, "Tell his wife she must forgive him." I called her over and told her what the Lord had said. She forgave him, and they wept in each other's arms. The Lord told him that he must go forth and preach the Gospel, and his wife also received the Holy Ghost.

The churches of Brazil needed teaching on the Body ministry, building each other up through the gifts of the Holy Ghost. Many of the people were spirit-filled but had not moved into the exercise of the gifts. Everywhere I went, therefore, I had to pray for people that the gift of prophecy would come forth. As the Spirit of God moved upon the people, even in homes, we saw the Lord amplify the gifts that were already in the lives of the Brazilian believers. Many prophesied and gave forth words of knowledge for the very first time in those meetings.

The people showed their love and appreciation

through numerous luncheons and dinners. We were
pulled into many homes and had wonderful fellowship
with the people. Many of the houses had tambourines
and guitars, and together we would sing hymns of praise
to God. We prayed for many people in their homes as
well. There were instantaneous healings of people who
were suffering from dizzy spells, instantaneous healings
of headaches, and many other miracles. God did some
very unusual things in those days.

One day, when they brought to me an elderly pastor
who had some problems, I shouted out in tongues while I
was praying for him. Brother Betenmiller said, "Oh, this
is too wonderful for words! You have just answered the
man in his own language (Portuguese) and given him the
answer to his problem."

I did some other unusual things too. I would never go
into a bar in my own home town, but in Brazil I was led to
do just that. I wanted to use every moment of the wonderful time God had given me. I went in, greeted
everyone and then began to speak to them about the love
of Jesus. I presented salvation through the blood of Jesus.
In one bar, there was a woman without hope, without
Christ, without health, without peace, sitting at the bar
drinking wine. When she turned, my heart went out to
her. When I had left the bar, I heard someone approach-
ing me. It was that lady. We couldn't converse, but she
put her arms around my waist and leaned against me
and, in that state, I led her to Jesus. I am positive that
somewhere in Brazil that woman is telling others how
God delivered her that day, for when He does a work He
does it thoroughly. Glory to His name!

We prayed for an unsaved man in another bar we
passed to receive the Lord, and he received with joy.

One day we went to pray for two elderly women near

the church. As we spoke to them, we saw them lifted out of despair and out of ill health, and we left them shouting and praising the Lord.

Brother Betenmiller lived by faith, which was wonderful because he understood my situation and knew how to pray prayers pertinent to such a life. We believed God together that there would be provision for his large family before he and his wife would take me into the Amazon region, which at first he was loath to do (because, he told me afterward, I had come in the wrong season, and it was much too hot for a foreigner in the Amazon). When I told him how two angels had commissioned me for that trip, he was content and no longer opposed the idea.

One day he said to me, "If you die in the heat of the Amazon, what will I tell Brother Heflin?"

"I will not die, and you will tell Brother Heflin that there has been great victory. In fact, I will tell him myself when I see him because God is leading me into victory and not into death."

When he got home that day after we had prayed, he found a large amount of money in his mailbox, more than enough to sustain his family while he was away. We were both thrilled at this provision. God never fails His work or His workers, and we went north into Brazil's interior.

I had told Brother Betenmiller that God had said for me to go to Ouro Preto, so he and his wife took me there. Ouro Preto is one of Brazil's most Catholic towns. The first day we entered the town, we went and stood in the town square. I looked up to Heaven and said, "Here I am, Lord."

I heard Him respond in my spirit, "And here I am also, my daughter."

We went into a restaurant and had a meal. We enjoyed it and paid the bill. Before we could leave, however, something very interesting happened. The proprietor, a lady, approached us and shouted very loudly, obviously under satanic power, "Get out of here and go home. You're not welcome here."

I stood to my feet, looked right into her eyes and, by the power of the Holy Ghost, said to her, "You did not invite me here, and I will not go home until God is finished with me in this place." She turned and walked away. It was another example of a blatant attack by the enemy.

Brother Betenmiller felt led to go to a Methodist church in Ouro Preto. The church had no pastor, and the daughter of the person who had built the church was trying to hold the congregation together. None of the members were Spirit-filled. I went to the door and knocked. Soon I realized that this was the place of which the Lord had spoken to me in my living room. The lady in charge wept and cried when she knew that God had sent someone all the way from America, a woman preacher, to bring them revival.

"I have prayed and prayed for someone to come and help us," she said. "We have been on our faces, fasting and praying and crying out to God for someone to come. I'll call everyone together." That night about forty people came, and all of them except one received the Holy Ghost, turning that little Methodist church into a power-house for God. I was so happy to see how God had answered the prayer of that woman. As I thought about it, I was overwhelmed with thanksgiving. She had cried out to God in the secret of her room, while I had laid before the Lord in Ashland, Virginia, and God had told me to go and help her. What a wonderful God we serve!

I thought of the Apostle Paul and his dream of the Macedonian man who said to him, "*Come over into Macedonia and help us*" (Acts 16:9). As I traveled about Brazil, I felt so many times like an answer to prayer for someone and knew that I wanted to live the rest of my life being just that, an answer to prayer for many.

There were two other churches in Ouro Preto. I preached in the Assemblies of God Church on Sunday morning and was ministering to the people in healing and the Holy Ghost, when the pastor interrupted. "I am very sorry," he said, "but I have to go now. I have an appointment to preach in another place. I must lock the church behind me." Everyone quickly exited, but a long line formed in the street, a line of sick and suffering people needing my prayers. When Jesus had been welcomed in the synagogue, He ministered there. When He was not able to minister there, He ministered to people wherever He found them. That day I again became God's street preacher and began ministering to that long line of hungry people where they stood in the street.

It began to rain, but the line did not shorten. People who had not been in the church came and got in line to be prayed for. Many lined up in the rain that day and received salvation and the Holy Ghost, speaking in tongues right there in the street. Before long we were being pulled into homes to pray for others. I remember sliding down one muddy, red hillside bank to reach the home of a needy family. All in the house were saved, healed and filled with the Holy Ghost. People were reaching out to touch us, reaching out to pull us this way and that. The power of God was so strong upon us that I understood the Ark of the Covenant where the presence of the Lord dwelled. God uses his ministers in that same way.

The crowds were growing so large that I couldn't reach out to everyone. Some people were gloriously saved and filled with the Holy Ghost before I could even touch them. Many of those who were praying began to see an-

gels about us and to cry out in amazement. Someone's
old uncle was standing there that day. An alcoholic, he
stood trembling and crying out. When the translator
asked him what was happening, he said that he had just
delivered his heart to Jesus because he saw an angel
standing with us.

Many sick people were wonderfully healed in those
moments.

That night we preached the Gospel in an Alliance
Church in Ouro Preto. Again many delivered their hearts
to Christ, and many were filled with the Holy Ghost.

By the time we left Ouro Preto all three of its evangelical churches had been turned upside down for the Lord,
and the whole town was talking about what God was
doing. When He tells us to go to a place, we have nothing
to fear. We can go with the knowledge that He goes with
us and will confirm His Word through us with signs and
wonders, just as He did in Bible days.

Before I left Ouro Preto, I bought an antique wrought-
iron oil lamp for my house. When I got back home, I hung
it in the living room, saying to the Lord, "This is the room
where you told me to go to Ouro Preto, and here is an oil
lamp which symbolizes the light of Your Word in that
place. I want You to know that any time You tell me to go
someplace, I will surely go."

He said, "And I surely will go with you." That lamp
hangs in my living room to this day.

We moved from town to town, from church to church,
across Brazil that year, ministering to the lovely people
we met in each place. The mountainous terrain was difficult to traverse, but God gave us strength and victory. My
heart is moved when I think of the many places we visited and of the many churches where we ministered, in

meetings of two thousand, three thousand and up to five thousand people.

In one church, we prayed for a feebleminded woman. Instead of my hands on her, Brother Betenmiller saw a vision of the scissors of God cutting all dead, putrefying flesh from her.

In these meetings, we prayed for people who needed deliverance from cigarettes and cigars, and God delivered them instantly.

I had been privileged to hear, many years before, in the suburbs of Philadelphia, a great missionary, Norman Grubb, the son-in-law of the famous C.T. Studd. He came to one of our meetings. He was himself a silver-haired pioneer by that time. I remember hearing him say, "Christ exists in you to meet every human need." As we walked through Brazil, I saw those words in action. He was indeed in us to meet the needs of the people.

The great miracles God was performing were softening the hearts of the people for His Word. During those months God gave me messages on holiness, on liberty in the Spirit, and on praise. I spoke on *Pastors After God's Own Heart* and had the sense that the pastors were being taught the ways of the Spirit. There is no doubt that pastors were being reinforced in their own minds on the message of holiness, one of the messages of the hour, along with the message of Jesus' soon return. Pastors knelt, weeping on the platforms as I prophesied over them the very issues of their hearts.

The pastors of Brazil preached holiness, but as in every country, many of the people did not want to live in holiness, did not want to walk in holiness, interior holiness, holiness of life – being faithful to one husband, being faithful to one wife, keeping the body clean from vices

and the other outward things that mean as much to God,
as well, among them, the modern idea that we should
wear apparel which shows our bodies. All these are scriptural admonitions, not man-made laws.

The pastors knew about these truths because the older
pastors had taught them, but modernism was creeping
in. Instead of modernism, we should call it what it is —
selfishness, willfulness. There is something in man that
makes him do what he wants to do. He wants to do what
he feels comfortable doing, and he always thinks that
God should be made comfortable with what man wants,
instead of man doing things God's way. But God is not
pouring out revival on people who want to do everything
their own way.

As the blind were being instantly healed and the lepers
instantly cleansed, as God's awesome power was being
demonstrated, God was softening the hearts of men and
women to get them to be obedient to His voice and His
Word.

Another of the powerful messages God gave me during those days was: *Ye Are the Salt of the Earth,* a challenge
to the church to live for Christ, to be more filled with the
Spirit than ever, to know that God was trusting them to
be a light in a dark world. So many times, when we criti-
cize and curse the darkness, it doesn't do any good. We
are not called to curse, we are called to bless. We are
called to dispel the darkness with our light. We must stop
hiding our lights in things that we want to do, the soft
life, the easy life. We have a Great Commission from God.

My body was weary at times, so weary that I felt I
could not go a step further. It was at those times that the
Holy Ghost stood up inside me, and I went on preaching
and laying hands on people. He is the message. He is the

life. He is the way. He is the truth. He is the health. He is the peace. And He is Himself the provision.

We needed God's miracles of provision in those days. When the team left me in Rio, they had generously turned their pockets inside out and left me with about US $400 to continue my mission, but before a week was out I had forgotten my purse and left it in a taxi. In the purse were my US $400 and my passport. I never saw the purse again. Brother Betenmiller felt it was God's way of show-ing all the Brazilian pastors that a person could really live by faith and that not every American was rich. Pastors took offerings for us when they had never given a cent to a foreign missionary before, and their generous offerings made possible the continuation of our mission.

Brother Betenmiller asked me if I was sure I wanted to go to the Amazon, and I, again, said yes, I was sure; so we went out and did some shopping for the trip. I particu-larly needed some sturdier shoes. I went down to the marketplace and stood by a sales lady. As the translator told her for me the things I wanted to buy, she began to tremble and weep. "What's the matter with her?" I asked.

"She's under conviction," Brother Betenmiller replied. "She's backslidden, and she sees in you what she used to be, what she has fallen from." It was my great pleasure to put my arms around that woman and to lead her back to Jesus.

While I was able to minister to many women, the women of Brazil also ministered to me. God had said to me, when I had to leave my own daughters for the trip, "I will give you many young women who will stand with you and love you like a mother." Everywhere I went women would come to me so lovingly, put their arms around me and stand with me. They wanted to carry my Bible for me, to carry my pocketbook, to help me in any way they could. They borrowed my dresses and used them as patterns to make me cotton dresses, suitable for the hot, humid climate. It was a joy for me to receive the love of these young women in the absence of my daughters.

Many young people from the Bible schools came to me. I prophesied over them, and many of them told me that what I said in prophecy was the very thing God had been dealing with them about. The process for them to find a place of ministry and/or financial support after graduation was to visit various places with their portfolio in hand. The portfolio had pictures of their evangelistic activities and newspaper reports of their meetings to impress people to help them. I spoke to them about trusting God and living by faith and assured them that when God calls, we need not wait. We can respond, knowing that He will surely provide. The idea of itinerating, going about asking people to support us, is an idea that has passed its usefulness. God is able to supply our needs when we get into the work He has ordained for us.

Through the prophecies the young people received confirmation to the work they were to be doing; and, time and time again, I saw them going off into the field, trembling a little, but trusting God. The Spirit of God is a pipeline of gold and oil straight from Heaven. God opened the valve and gave to each young person the message he or she needed at the moment.

This ministry was not limited to the young people. Many of the elderly pastors who had been praying for revival for a long time heard about what was happening and called for us to come to their churches. It humbled me to see seasoned pastors, some in their fifties and sixties, others in their eighties, kneel in front of me like children, weeping to receive something from God. One pastor told me in Portuguese (and I understood it all without the aid of the translator), "When you came here, I knew that you were no ordinary missionary." He was speaking of the miracle working power of God. Could anything in this life be more wonderful than hearing God speak and of being a voice crying in the wilderness: *Make straight the way of the Lord?*

The devil didn't like my being in Brazil. Many times we were confronted by the *Macumba* worshipers, devil worshipers. We had to deal with another cult, the followers of a woman called *La Manja*. In her photos she looks amazing like the Virgin Mary in a blue and white gown. Since Mary is called *The Star of the Sea* by the Catholics of Brazil, and since this woman says that she rises out of the sea, many people follow her. Her followers go down to the seaside in white dresses and white turbans, then imbibe alcoholic beverages before they begin their evil worship. We testified to many of those followers of the love of Jesus.

One morning I was talking to a street vendor who had a portrait of *La Manja* on his little cart. "She cannot save you," I told him. "She cannot heal you; she cannot help you; she cannot get you to Heaven. She is an evil spirit." At that moment a wind came up and knocked the picture flat on his cart, and I could see fear in the man's eyes. "You see," I told him, "even Heaven testifies to you that what I am telling you is true."

Many times we were asked by home owners to come to their homes and pray because of the devil worshipers that had set up a place of worship near them or (in the case of apartment dwellers) in the apartment next to them or over them. We were told that within a week or two of our prayers those places had closed. Our Lord prevails!

We had a very wonderful experience in Joa Pasoa. After we had been up to Recife, we went on to a place called Campiña Grande, in the state of Pernambuco. It was the 50th anniversary of the Assemblies of God Church in Brazil, having been founded in 1924. Pastors had come from many places to celebrate. Much of the program was made a long time in advance, and there were very special speakers. A woman had never spoken. One of the leaders, however, had heard what God was doing through our ministry, the miracles that were taking place, and so they allowed me to speak twice in the five-day celebration. Some amazing healings took place there.

In many cities of Brazil I had opportunity to minister to the Jews living there. I made it a point to visit the synagogues and talk and minister to the Rabbis. I also made it a point to visit the offices of the Jewish Federation and to talk to the heads of Jewish agencies. I prophesied over them and left them weeping and loving Christians because I told them things in prophecy that only God knew about them, things that only He *could* know about them.

No committee that is not led by the Holy Ghost can bring about a good relationship between Jews and Christians. This miracle can come about only by the Spirit of God; but He does it so easily; for we are both people who know the fellowship of suffering for the sake of the Word of God. How could there anything but love and unity between us in these days?

I met Jewish people in other places. One man I met in a library, looking for a map, and I prayed for him right there.

God told me to go to Sao Paulo, and I went quickly. There I spoke to many Jewish people. In the Jewish Federation there, a large group of young people gathered to hear me speak about Israel and Russia. As I was speak-

ing, the women began to cry. They were rubbing their
arms. I asked them what was happening. They said, "We
feel something like needles raining on our arms."

"That is the witness of the Holy Spirit, *Ruach ha ko desh*
[in Hebrew]" I told them. That thrilled their hearts. Two
things speak to the Jews these days: a love for the land of
Israel and a love for the Jewish language. When you
speak Hebrew to a Jewish person, they know you love
them. The Lord alone is responsible to reveal Himself,
and He is able to make Himself known to those who hunger for His presence. We can only speak to them with
love and power. The rest is in His hands. We must speak
to them with such love, however, that they are left con-
templating our words.

We were invited to the home of a Jewish family. We
spoke to them of what God was doing in Russia, and they
were thrilled.

We spoke to a group of Jewish people in the home of
one of the women we met. For several hours I talked to
them of Old Testament prophecies and of more recent
prophecies that had come in our church concerning the
Jews and about the Russian trips.

A certain town in southern Brazil was well known as a
summering place for the Jews. I felt led to go there. Arriving at a hotel there I recognized some of the men in the
lobby as being Jews. I went up to them, telling them that I
was a Christian minister sent by the Lord to speak with
them. Because my last name is of German origin, there
was some initial fear. "You're German, aren't you?" they
asked.

"I am an American," I answered, "a Pentecostal minister, and God has sent me here to speak with you. I love
you, and I love Israel, and it is because God loves you." I
had nothing to give me favor with these men except the

witness of the Spirit of God. Without the favor which
God gives, as a result of our having favor with Him, we
would be powerless to influence others. I saw the Spirit
of God melt their hearts. They invited me into a hidden
synagogue they had built right there in the hotel. It was a
great privilege to be there on the Lord's behalf and I
spoke very openly of the need for Jews everywhere to
return home to Israel. As I spoke to them of God's purposes for the end-time, I felt such marvelous fulfillment
of my purpose in Brazil. After we sang some Israeli songs
together, I departed, leaving them with the assurance
that they had been visited by God.

Because of our visits to the synagogues, there was a
new interest in Jesus among the Jewish communities, a
new expectancy for the coming of Messiah. They were
equally excited about the return of the Jews to Israel and
the role of Israel in the last days. Many of the Jews of
Brazil began to pray in those days for the release of their
fellow Jews from Russia.

The Brazilian pastors were very moved by my ministry
to the Jewish people. They had never seen such, and it
was widely talked about among them. In all his thirty
years as a pastor in the Assemblies of God, Brother
Betenmiller had also never seen such ministry to the
Jews. In the churches we visited, he felt compelled to tell
the other preachers what God was doing, and they too
were thrilled.

Word got back to Rio and to the leaders of the church in
Sao Cristavao. "They explained it this way," my pastor
later told me. "Imagine, not only a healing campaign, not
only a salvation campaign, and not only a campaign in
which the people are being filled with the Holy Ghost
and delivered. To top it all off, the Jews are being
reached." I wondered what all the fuss was about. I was

just doing what God had trained me to do. This is what God had been preparing me for all my life. When He says "Fullness," He means it.

God was good to send me encouragement when I needed it most in my months in Brazil. Some wonderful letters from my pastor and from other missionaries in South America helped me during this time. At one point, I was joined by Sister Bessie Olmstead, one of the great women evangelists of the Assemblies of God of Canada. Her prophetic word greatly enhanced the meetings. It was like a beautiful painting. From her years of experiencing the love of God, such beautiful tints came forth in the prophetic word.

We were joined another week by Brother Harold McDougal and Brother Bert Colosaga from the Camp in Quito. Their wisdom, grace and Christ-likeness brought forth wonderful results in every meeting and encouraged me much.

At every turn, however, I felt cradled in the arms of prophecy. When I needed extra guidance, there would be someone in the back of the church, some little lady or some young person who would stand and speak out loud in Portuguese. Brother Betenmiller would translate the message into English for me, and it was the Lord speaking to me directly. Some of the people had visions and saw an angel standing beside me and many other visions that were meaningful only to me.

As I walked about Brazil in the glory cloud, I felt that it was my inheritance. I was welcomed in every place. However, in one church, a deacon felt that he simply could not stand for an American or a woman to speak in his church. When we arrived he asked Brother Betenmiller, "Is that the woman?"

"Yes," he answered.

"Well, bring her in the back door, not the front," he said. "We don't want her here."

So, humbly I went around to the back door. After a marvelous message and a marvelous moving of the Spirit (in which many were saved and many were healed), the old man ran out after us. He was still angry about a woman being allowed to preach in his church, but he felt that he simply had to speak by the Spirit. He shouted in our faces; but it was not him, it was the Holy Ghost, turning him into another man. His words were: "I say unto thee, thou art welcome here. Thou art welcome here. Thou art welcome here." God knows how to change men's hearts. I have never feared to walk in any place where the Spirit leads me.

Many of the young girls who attended the meetings wept when they saw a woman preaching for the first time. They had wanted to serve the Lord for a long time. The only way for them to serve the Lord, they were taught, was to marry a preacher. After I returned home, I wept and travailed much over Brazilian women, praying that when I next returned I would find change. "If Jesus, Who gave the Holy Ghost for service and for holiness, didn't want women to preach or serve the Lord in a public capacity," I assured them, "He would not have filled them with the Holy Ghost." Now I could only pray that my message took root.

When God would do miracles, I would dance a little in praise. I quickly noticed, however, that my dancing seemed to turn people off. I inquired and found that dancing was not appreciated in any of the churches of Brazil. That mystified me, and I determined that if God was doing miracles I must at least jump about a little and let Him know how much I appreciated what He was doing.

Now and then I would mention joy in the Spirit and dancing as a manifestation of that joy in the Spirit. When I did this, however, I could sense the same wall go up in those to whom I was ministering. Dancing was, to them, only worldly and of the devil. Finally I realized that there was something wrong that I was not understanding. These people loved God; of that I was sure. What was I missing?

One day I leaned over and asked a young Brazilian evangelist sitting on the platform if I could see his Bible. I turned to the 150th Psalm, and there I discovered a problem. The Portuguese translation of the Bible had completely taken out the words *"Praise the Lord in the dance."* It grieved me to think that a whole generation of people would not hear all the truth in this matter, for dancing is an important truth for revival, and an important truth for life and liberty in the Holy Ghost. Since that time, I have prayed that God would take care of this omission.

Were the words of the angel fulfilled? We traveled up the Amazon River Basin, and arrived at Macapa Island and a large Indian church. While the miracles were taking place, an elderly pastor stood to his feet and said in a loud voice, "Surely this woman must be an angel sent from God." This confirmed to me what the angel had foretold.

A notable thing happened in another place. One Sunday afternoon the pastors came to me and asked me to go to a house of a family in which the father and mother were Christians. In the back of their little Indian hut was another tiny shack built of bamboo. I had to stand up on an ant hill to be able to look through the barred window. There I saw a demon-possessed man dressed in filthy pajamas. As I stood up on that nest, I spoke to him and asked him if the would be willing to serve the Lord if he were free. With a fierce look in his eyes, he signaled to me with a violent shake of the head, that he would not.

I have found that we are powerless to do anything in these cases except the Spirit move. The Lord told me, "Speak to the man, not the demons." I did. I began to tell him what a terrible place Hell is and that this was his destination if he insisted on serving the devil. Then I spoke of the glories and the joys of Heaven's reward if he served the Lord.

Then, with my whole being crying out for the soul of that man, I asked him again if he would change his mind and serve the Lord. This time he answered affirmatively. The moment he said yes, he took himself out of the hands of the devil. I laid hands on him through the grill and prayed, "In the name of Jesus Christ of Nazareth, devil, leave him."

The pastor shouted, "Open the door," and someone behind us prophesied loudly in Portuguese, "This day I liberate you."

The door opened, and that man came out of that tiny shack for the first time in seven years, and he was in his right mind. It was one of the greatest miracles I ever witnessed. Some years later I inquired about the young man. Brother Betenmiller told me that he is still going to church and still serving the Lord. To God be the glory!

Before I left Brazil, someone who spoke English said to me, "I have never seen it before as I have seen it in these days." I thought that about summed up my trip.

I needed to make reservations for the return trip, and I began to wonder very early just when I should go back. During the New Year's Eve holiday, I had the opportunity to sit before a television set at the Pessoa's home.

(Although I was just as happy in huts, I found that the Lord was just as pleased to put me in mansions.) I don't remember what the program was, but in the course of the program they showed a calendar for March of the following year. I never knew why, but I got my answer. The date *March 21st* lit up, over and over again. I knew the Spirit was telling me to be home on that date, and I made my reservations.

In one city, one of the brothers in the church was a member of a highly-placed intelligence organization in the government. He was spirit-filled and took it upon himself to get me a new passport to replace the one I lost in the taxi.

After all the miracles, after all the victories, I arrived home in Ashland on schedule. What I didn't know was that Brother Heflin would come in from Australia that same day. Other missionaries also arrived the same day from other parts of the world, each of us led to return home on the exact same day. God has a sure timetable.

As I look back on that first visit to Brazil, I am thankful. It is impossible for me to enumerate everything the pastors did for me: the phone calls, the recommendations, the joy with which they spoke sometimes, before or after I did, about the greater flowing of the prophecy in the church or the reiteration of the holiness message. "From this day forth," they declared, "we will have more holiness in the church in Brazil; for what this woman has told us is real. We see, as never before, that the life of holiness brings the power of God, and we are determined to have it here in Brazil." God has blessed those men and lifted them up because of their stand. That denomination gained three million souls in the next four years.

The night I arrived home from Brazil, and all the other missionaries arrived as well, we were together in the church, and the Lord spoke to us and said, "You have gone out individually, but now I send you out two by two," and that night He prophetically named people in the service who were to go out two by two. Within ten days time, in these meetings, all the money was raised for the tickets needed for their trips. What a miracle! There is no finer mission board than that of the Father, the Son and the Holy Ghost.

Chapter 7

Australia

It is God that avengeth me, and subdueth the people under me.   Psalm 18:47

I was praying one summer and expecting a fresh vision of where the Lord would have me to go when camp was over. One of the speakers that year was a brother from Australia. After he preached, he began to minister to many people around the altar. When he came to me, he laid his hands on me and began to prophesy: "Behold, I call you to a dark people sunk in the bonds of sin and animism. I send you forth and give you great victory among them." As time went on, I began to feel that God meant the aboriginal people of Australia. I felt like their spiritual mother. As I continued to fast and pray for them, the Lord gave me the name of a person, someone who seemed to be a tribal leader.

When the proper time came, and after I had consulted with my pastors, I went to the travel agent and made arrangements for myself and the traveling companion the Lord had given me, an English lady. We first went to

India, then to Singapore and from there to Darwin, Australia. We found Darwin to be a very hot place — all year round. They had two seasons, wet and dry, but the temperature stayed high through both seasons. We arrived in November.

An Australian man who had also visited the camp and heard of our burden gave us the name of a pastor there. Darwin was nowhere near the area where the black tribal people of Australia lived, a place called Fitzroy Crossing, but we felt led to stop there first. We arrived at the airport in the middle of the night. I was not about to call a pastor at that hour, so we stayed in the airport until seven in the morning, then called him.

The man was very gracious and came to pick us up, but it was immediately apparent that he didn't know what to think of an American lady and an English lady coming to his country for missionary work. As he neared his part of the city, the Spirit of God came upon me and I began to prophesy. He pulled to the side of the road and stopped the car. As he did so, he broke into weeping as the Holy Ghost told him everything he had said to God in his prayer closet when He first called him to preach. When he had composed himself, we continued on our way.

We met his wife and his teenage children, and they put us in the master bedroom for our two-week stay. Very early in our visit we sensed a very great need, not only in the church but in the home. It didn't take long to discover that a young married woman was also living in the home and was known to be the pastor's girlfriend. I had never been in such a situation before, but I knew one thing: Jesus was the answer to it all, and He had put me directly into that situation to deal with it in holiness.

At first I only prayed privately and travailed for the situation. The pastor sensed that God had sent us and that we had a word for him and his people. He began to call the church members together. I overheard him saying on the phone, "You must come to the meeting tonight. The gift of prophecy is in operation." I could sense the excitement of the people who had been hurt by the situation. People aren't blind. As I met the church members later and preached to them over the next week, it seemed to me that many of them had come out of similar situations, so that they were not quick to judge or blame their pastor. While they were heartsick about it, they were hoping for God's resolution.

The wife of the pastor had been deeply hurt and needed our help. "Does God want to break up my marriage?" she asked us. "Should I give up and let this other woman take over?"

"Absolutely not!" I assured her. "God never desires the destruction of a marriage. This is the result of sin. You must look to Jesus this week and see what God will do." In prophecy God told her not to give her place to another, and she felt very encouraged.

As much as any of these, the pastor himself needed our help. He needed rebuke and correction, but I knew that I could not use the pulpit of the church, as some do, mixing correction with the exhortation of the Word of God for the whole body. The pulpit is not a sounding board to keep us from doing our duty to speak directly to those who are in sin. The pulpit is to be used for preaching *Christ and Him crucified*. Usually correction must be aimed at an individual or a small group of individuals, not at the whole church.

As for the other woman, I found it very difficult to find anything to say to her. The Word of God judged her guilty, and I hated the hurt she had caused so many. The first time I found her alone, my advice to her was to, "Get

out, and leave the pastor alone," which she did not seem
inclined to do. Once, when prophecy was going forth in
the assembly, the pastor brought this woman to me and
asked if I didn't have a word for her. "No," I answered,
"because she has not obeyed the plain Word of God." I
wanted to be merciful to everyone involved, but truth
had to prevail.

There were others who needed our help, for instance a
policeman had been called to preach but was now backslidden, and his wife was twice as backslidden as he was.

I knew that if God had brought me there for that time
He knew that I could handle the situation in the power of
His Spirit and His Word. The word that came forth to the
church was a word of salvation, a word of healing, an
uplifting word, a call to holiness.

I began to preach on holiness and God began to re-call
His people to His standards of living. At night, after the
service, a woman would come and sit beside me on the
sofa in the pastor's living room, just to hear more of that
teaching and just to be near that anointing. As I spoke,
she sat beside me weeping. By the end of the week, that
woman had a new wardrobe, clothes befitting the wife of
a man called to preach the Gospel, and she had been
totally transformed, turned into a very different woman.
Others were transformed, giving themselves over completely to the move of God.

A policeman had been scheduled to work one night of
the campaign, but he wanted to attend the meetings, so
he asked a friend to fill in for him. That friend, upon
answering the first call of the night, a domestic quarrel in
the home of an aboriginal couple, was shot dead. "Being
in church saved my life," he told me. "I want to show my
gratitude by serving God the rest of my life. I am prepared to preach anywhere He chooses to send me."

God had brought us for other reasons. Missionaries of the Methodist Church who were serving in the outlying islands, men and women who loved God, were very eager to be filled with the Holy Ghost. They were horrified, however, by the sinful life of this pastor and would not come to his church. They invited us to dinners in their homes, and we were able to minister to them, each of them being filled with the Spirit. They were very eager to hear end-time teachings and to know what God was doing in Russia, in Israel and around the world. They were encouraged and lifted up and I am confident that they went on to light many revival fires themselves.

The church was revived and, as people who had left the church began to hear about the wonderful things God was doing, about the prophetic word and the message of the end-times, they came back. Within ten days, the church had tripled in size.

While we were in Darwin, I shared with the people our vision of going to the aboriginals. I hadn't been aware that our tickets would not take care of that side trip (over to the town of Derby, in the desert, and then down to Aboriginal territory, far away) and that it would cost us US $400 extra to make the trip, but God knew and He moved on those people to help us. Within a few days, with a very small attendance, the money was raised. God will always reward those people for their faithfulness. In their new-found consecration, they started their own little mission, and we were unexpectedly their missionaries.

Before we ever left the airport in Darwin, we experienced great opposition, opposition from an unexpected source. The head of one of Australia's evangelical missions was in the airport. "I hear that you are going down to Fitzroy Crossing," he said to us sternly.

"Yes," I answered.

"I don't want you to go," he said. "You're not welcome there. You're very Pentecostal."

"Yes, that's true," I answered, "but God has told us to go there."

"Well, I don't want you at our mission there," he retorted.

"I'm not going to your mission," I answered. "We plan to stay at a hotel."

"There's only one hotel down there, and it's full of drunks," he said.

"Well, that's alright," I answered. "We don't drink, so we'll be safe."

I could only hope that Jesus would revive him, to be used in the important work of the end-times. And we boarded our plane for Derby.

We had to spend the night at a hotel there in Derby, and we took advantage of the time to pray and intercede before God to fill that place with His glory. We have heard since then that there are some wonderful spirit-filled churches now that did not exist before our visit. We left the next night for Fitzroy Crossing.

While we were waiting in Derby for the plane, millions of stars were encrusted in the Australian night sky, stars that we never see in our Northern Hemisphere. We shouted with joy to see them. Considering the opposition that was behind us and the unknown that lay before us, the God of Creation, just as He had pulled Job out of his difficulties, used the beauty of the Universe to lift us up as well, and we praised Him for the strength of His creation. We spoke in tongues for about an hour and a half, until our throats were barely able to utter more sound when the plane finally arrived.

As we landed at Fitzroy Crossing and stepped off that

little plane, we felt the heat of the day, a heat that we have never experienced before or since. It was 125° (Fahrenheit) that day. The mission truck came for some other aboriginals, and the mission truck went. We had been told that we were not welcome at the mission, but we were not duly concerned. God had another work for us to do.

I had one name, the name of that tribal leader the Holy Spirit had given me in prayer in my room in Ashland, Virginia. The name was George. The problem was that I had mentioned George to the head of that missionary organization who had not wanted us to come, and he had said that George lived with them. So how would I meet and minister to George when I was forbidden to step foot on the mission where he lived because I was Pentecostal? I began praying seriously for George and his tribal clan.

The hotel in Fitzroy Crossing by the gas pumps was very small and very hot. I was so happy to find that our sparse little room was air-conditioned. We never seek luxuries, but God knows when we need air-conditioning.

I was shocked to find someone waiting for us in our room. It was a very young missionary girl. She was dressed in brief attire and had her hair cut off like a boy's. She couldn't have been more than twenty-one or two. She was flippant and hostile toward us. She had been briefed by the head of the mission by telephone that two Pentecostal missionary women wanted to see George. "It would be better to take George and his wife to their hotel room for the interview," he said. "Whatever you do, don't let those Pentecostals set foot on the mission. They have false doctrine." She came now, leading George and his wife by the hand.

God's desire for George was to fill him with the Holy Ghost, to cause him to grow up, so that he could be the head and not the tail, enabling him to get out from under the thumb of people who named the name of Jesus but who preached a powerless Christ.

"This is the man you want to see," she told me, "but let me warn you. We don't want false doctrine at our mission."

"Sit down," I said to her. "I don't have any false doctrine." She was on my territory, so she had no choice but to sit down.

"Thea, could you please fix this young lady some tea," I asked, "and keep her occupied for a little while."

I took George and his wife by the hand and said, "George, are you the leader of your people?"

"Yes ma'am," he answered. "There are only about forty of us left in our tribe, but I am the leader."

"God sent me to talk to you," I told him. "God sent me to help you. Tell me what is happening."

George was overwhelmed to think that Jesus talked to someone on the other side of the world about him. He was so hungry for more of God, and his wife was so soft and yielded that it was a joy to lead them into the deeper things of the Lord.

"Sister," he said, "my wife and I adopted a baby recently, one of the first adoptions in our tribe." (Some member of the tribe had died and left a baby.) "Something happened to the baby. I don't understand why. We loved and cared for the baby so much, but our baby died. When the baby died, everyone turned on us. They said it was our fault, that we had done something to the baby. They accused us of putting a spell on the child. This broke my heart, and you can't imagine the pressure we have been under among our own people."

"George," I answered, "when tribal traditions and tribal pressures come up against the Word of the living

God, that tradition has to go. You did nothing wrong. You took on the care of an abandoned child, and the death was not your fault. Jesus has called me to tell you that He loves you and that you must receive His Spirit and lead your tribe into the fullness of God."

He was so excited with this news. "I want that," he said.

I noticed the mission girl sitting there and knew that, if she witnessed George and his wife being filled with the Spirit, she would not rest until she had convinced them that the experience was not of God. "I will see you later," I said. "I will be here for a while."

As they were leaving that night, I put an offering into George's hand and said to him, "God told me to honor you as the head of your tribe and to place this money into your hand." He was very appreciative.

Early the next morning we went out to have a look at the place. We saw clouds of beautiful white parrots and pink and gray parrots flying overhead. It was gorgeous territory. Nearby, in a dry gulch, there were thousands of these birds. There were many unusual and interesting plants to see as well. Then we went back to our room to pray.

Even with the air-conditioner running at full blast, it was still hot in the room, so we lay on the cool floor for a while in our slips and prayed in tongues and worshiped the Lord, interceding for George and his wife and for his people, for revival in all the tribes in the area. We had no idea what our next move was. Then suddenly, God spoke to me and said, "Get up and go outside." We dressed again and went outside. There, in back of the hotel stood George with a friend. "Oh, Sister," he said, "They told me at the mission that you had gone away. I was heartbroken."

"George," I said, "I came here at the request of the Lord to lay hands on you to receive the Holy Ghost. Let's do that right now." Right there we prepared to lay our hands on them and pray.

The heat of the day was unbearable, and I suddenly began to feel faint. Then I remembered the word of prophecy I had received from a Canadian sister just before I left America: *"I have not called you to faint, but I have called you to go forth and accomplish that which I have called you to do."* I felt refreshed immediately. As I laid hands on George and his friend, they began to speak in tongues, receiving the baptism of the Holy Ghost.

After we had prayed together for a time, I told him, "Now, go home, George, and preach to your people that Jesus saves, Jesus heals and Jesus fills with the Holy Ghost. Never again will another child in your tribe sicken and die. In the name of Jesus, He gives you power to heal the sick."

In that moment the power of God shot through his body, and he went on his way praising God, ready to preach the Gospel to his people. We have heard of wonderful revival among those tribes in Australia.

We went back to our rooms, got some tea, and lay down again on the floor in the burning heat to intercede for the people of the area. A few hours later the Lord said to us, "Get up and go outside." We got dressed again and went out. "This time," the Lord said, "stand in front of the shop."

That "shop" was a liquor store. There we saw a great crowd of aboriginals waiting for the store to open. They had just received their government checks and were ready to spend the total week's income on liquor.

Wives huddled with their babies beside nearby trees, sad that the income intended to feed them would be used instead for drink. Out from this great crowd of people came a large black man with a bushy afro-like haircut and approached us. "Hello Sister," he said, "I saw you on the plane coming down."

"Oh yes," I remembered then.

He told us that his name was Johnny.

"Are you an elder of your tribe?" I asked.

"I am the chief of my tribe," he answered, and told us what tribe it was.

"Then you must have a burden for your people," I suggested.

Johnny was beginning to feel the presence of God, something he had never felt before, and his eyes began to light up.

"God wants you to evangelize your people," I told him.

"Well, I have tried to help them," he answered, "and that's why I'm sick. When I saw you, yesterday, I was just returning from the hospital. These men will stand here and drink until they fall down. I try to get them away from here. I get the police to come and take some of them into protective custody for their own good. I drag some of those who have fallen into the shade of the trees. If they keep drinking they eventually get hurt. Some of them kill or get killed. My people misunderstood what I was doing. They called me an Uncle Tom and told me I was only helping the white policemen. They kicked me nearly to death and damaged one of my kidneys, and I had to be hospitalized."

"Johnny," I said, "stand here with us a moment. Now, in the name of Jesus Christ, receive ye the Holy Ghost." At that moment the Holy Ghost shook him from head to foot. God healed his damaged kidney, and he went off into the crowd shouting and leaping and praising God. I understand that he is still working faithfully for his people.

We went back to our room, lay down on the floor and rejoiced and interceded some more. We wept for the tribal people. Then the Lord spoke to us one more time, "Get up and go outside." We got dressed and went out. "Stand, this time, by the gas pumps," the Lord directed us. So, we took our position by the gas pumps, waiting for the next miracle the Lord would do.

Before long an old car pulled up. It was covered with the dust of the road. In the front was a young man and his wife, and lying naked in the back seat was a little baby, suffering from the intense heat. The couple was on the road and looking for a church that might help them to reach their next destination, and they could not speak English, only Spanish.

I had learned Spanish, you will recall, to be able to read the letters of my South American cousins, and through my travels in South America; my companion had learned Spanish through her long years of faithful service in Asunción, Paraguay, with the South American Mission. We stood and ministered to this couple, prophesying over them in Spanish. We gave them some money and the address of our friends in Darwin, and they went on praising the Lord. We felt that our work was accomplished, in barely a day and a half, and we flew out the next morning.

We went back to the church in Darwin and delivered a few more messages, confident that God was going to resolve many situations. We left them in revival.

We went on to work with another Pentecostal church. Together we preached in the streets of the city, and we preached in the trailer parks. We preached in the caravan park. The place was known as the Sodom and Gomorrah of Australia. Many of the unmarried girls in the high school were pregnant. Most of the couples in the trailer park were not married to each other but were living in sin. I told them that it was sin and that they would have to answer to God because Jesus was coming soon. Some laughed, but others became serious. Some of them refused to believe that what they were doing was sin and even bragged about their life-style. I wept over them and saw souls come to Christ.

The church was revived; missionaries were revived; the aborginals were revived. That weekend, when we were boarding our plane for America, I stood at the airport with my hands upraised and besought God one last time to undertake in that place. "I have done everything I could," I prayed. "I have gone where You sent me and said what You gave me to say. Oh God, shake this town for Your glory." Two weeks later, at midnight on Christmas Eve, the news swept round the world that a devastating hurricane had passed over the city of Darwin, Australia. Just as God had given a sinful world its greatest gift on Christmas Eve, He now gave some unrepentant Darwinites a judgment gift.

As the terrible winds swept over the city, homes were ripped apart, caved in and turned upside down. The worst devastation was in the caravan park where I had labored with tears. It was in that caravan park that I had met the grieving husband of the woman involved with the preacher. He had asked, "Is there any hope? Is there any help?"

I could only answer, "Trust in God. Sin will not last forever. God must judge it." He threw himself on God.

Now, God lifted the caravans up and threw them down the cliff under darkness of night. They landed in the ocean filled with stinging, poisonous jelly fish. If the people of that place could have escaped the plunge down the cliff, they could never have escaped the sting of the jelly fish. They perished. What a fearful thing!

God had spoken. If we answer with a humble heart when God speaks to us, we need never experience such wrath. Oh, that men everywhere would hear and obey His voice!

When the storm had passed, forty-four thousand inhabitants of the city were left homeless, yet another scar on the Australian city that had the dubious distinction of being the only town bombed twice by the Japanese during World War II.

We later received many letters from people thanking us for coming to their town. A group of the believers were praying in a house when the storm struck. As they saw the roof lift up, they interceded in tongues and were saved as the roof settled back into its place and remained.

The young man I had prophesied over, who allowed the Lord to transform him and his wife, went all over Australia preaching and giving news interviews concerning the power of God in his life.

The preacher who was going his own way, sad to say, was stricken by a near-fatal kidney ailment and moved to another place.

We left Darwin on a small plane that would land for a few minutes at a tiny aboriginal settlement known as Manangrida. The airport was little more than a cow pasture, but it served as the center for the black settlements of the North. The Lord spoke to me that I had only a few minutes as the plane prepared to take off again to meet someone important. "I will use you to bring revival here," He told me. Near the tiny airfield shack stood a strong black man with his sweet-faced wife. I knew that this was the man I was to meet.

We disembarked from the plane and went over to the little wooden rail fence where some people were waiting. As we got nearer, I put my hand out toward him, and he actually ran toward us. "Hello Sister," he said, as if he knew by the Spirit that we had been sent by God.

This man was well-known for his Christian testimony, for his kindness, and for his wisdom. He was the judge over ten tribes.

"Who are you?" he asked.

I told him who I was and that I was sent by God, and he introduced me to his wife.

"God said to tell you that He is going to revive your people," I said. That news thrilled him.

His wife, it turned out, had suffered an accident and had some brain damage and memory loss. "Will you pray for her?" he asked.

We laid hands on her and she was healed by the hand of God right then and there.

We only had time to get his name and address before we boarded the plane for our continuing flight, but we left him rejoicing like we had conducted a revival crusade of several weeks duration. It took the Spirit of God all of five minutes to perform it.

We flew next to another small airport in the north of Australia, several hundred miles to the east of Manangrida. The plane landed there just for a moment. I got out again and went over to the railing. There, in a crowd of about thirty-five aboriginal people, was a man that stood out to me. I went up to him and shook his hand. He told me that he was a pastor there. "God wants to bring revival in this place," I told him. "I don't think I will be back this way again, but God told me to say to you, 'Receive revival, in the name of the Lord Jesus Christ. I am visiting your people.' " The man was thrilled and started praising God.

I never saw him again, but I later heard that such revival had come to the place that people were praying fourteen hours a day. By faith, we can decree the will of God for a place, and it will come to pass.

The next year again the Lord put the Aboriginal people in my heart, and I went up to Manangrida — with Sister Jane Lowder, this time. We met our friend again and found that his wife had been totally healed since the time we prayed for her at the airport the year before. He arranged meetings for us and a small house where we could stay.

I did the cooking. One evening, as the smell of the cooking wafted down from our little house, this brother and some of his people came down. Together we enjoyed great pots of rice with squid and pumpkin, vegetables and onion. It was lovely fellowship.

As we prayed together, God led us into the homes of the people. We walked from house to house, ministering to each family; and we experienced great revival and marvelous healings. We were asked to have teaching sessions, and many responded. During those days we saw many wonderful healings.

As we continued our journey, we landed at Groote Island Airport. Because of the mine there, entrance to the area is restricted, but somehow our tickets took us there. When it was discovered that we did not have official permission to be there, we were granted only twenty-four hours.

The local Episcopalian priest, who was spirit-filled, was sent to see why we were there. "I know exactly why you are here," he said when he arrived, and he began to bring people to us for personal ministry. This continued all afternoon. Bodies were healed; marriages were

healed; prophecy went forth; God did great works in our
short time in that place.

Another year Brother Heflin Jr. was scheduled to go
out to Australia with a male companion. Sister Jane and I
wanted so badly to go, but two single women couldn't
travel with two men, so we determined to stay home and
fast and pray. I felt led to fast on nothing but water. It
became quite hard on the thirteenth day. Later Mother
Heflin told me, "You looked like death on the thirteenth
day. I was afraid for you and prayed." I am grateful for
her prayers because God gave me strength and I continued fasting for twenty-seven days. Long hours into the
night I could be found in my room on the floor travailing
and weeping for the tribal people of Australia. I was believing for revival among all the aboriginal groups there.
I expect to see a great complement of black Australians in
Heaven one day.

When twenty-seven days had passed and I couldn't
fast any longer, Sister Ruth Heflin made a surprise visit
from Israel. She was on her way to some meeting and
said she had no intention of stopping by the camp, but
the Lord changed her plans. That morning, when she
walked into the prayer room, she looked at me and said,
"You have been fasting, haven't you?"

"Yes, I have," I answered.

"You have a burden," she continued, "and that burden
is for the Aboriginal nations of Australia."

"Yes, but we couldn't go because the men were going."

"Come here," she said. At the same moment she called
two others over and began to prophesy over the three of
us: "You shall go forth." As it turned out, she had something to do in Australia herself, so she took us with her.
Someone gave us their savings of $3,000 for our fares.

We spent a night or two in Newcastle where Brother

Heflin and his companion were ministering. Then, leaving Sister Ruth behind to take care of her business, the three of us ladies flew on to Manangrida. We contacted the authorities of one of the major Christian denominations there and sought permission to conduct meetings in their church. They refused because we were Pentecostal, and they did not believe in speaking in tongues. God told us to go. "My daughter," the Lord said to me, "you do not need a church to preach in. You will walk in the streets like I walked in the streets of Jerusalem, and I will walk with you."

We stopped at a place where men were gathered under a tree, gambling and drinking. One of the men had a withered arm. It had been paralyzed since he fell from a truck, and he could not move it. We laid hands on him and prayed the prayer of faith, and God loosed that man's arm as he stood before us. He lifted it up and moved it about. As a result, he confessed the Lord as his Savior.

Another man, famous among the Aboriginals because he had written several books, had tuberculosis. We prayed for him and he was healed instantly.

Continuing up the street, we came to a man laying on a cot outside his house. "Who are you?" he asked.

"We are preachers," we answered, "come in the name of Jesus to pray for you and see you healed." We laid hands on him and prayed. Later that afternoon, we saw the man following us. He had been totally healed the moment we prayed.

We walked up another pathway. A tall Aboriginal man saw us coming and came down partway to meet us. On his shoulder he carried his six-year-old daughter. She had been born with feet like flippers, and she had never walked. I wept as I took her off his shoulder and set her on her feet. "In the name of Jesus Christ of Nazareth," I cried, "be healed." As we departed, she was still standing on her own strength, waving joyfully. She was healed and able to walk for the first time in her life. The fact is that every person we touched in that place was healed, every single one.

We heard that there was another missionary lady living there, so we decided to visit her. She, however, was very hostile toward us. She didn't believe that healing was for today and wanted nothing at all to do with us. Not only did she not give us the customary tea, she didn't even want to speak with us. She stayed in her house during our time there and missed the revival God was sending in the streets. We prayed for her ministry with love.

We came upon a man standing in the way. His heart was so severely damaged, his wife told us, that it could not even be replaced. "Please pray for him," she pleaded. One of us got behind him and another in front and an arc of the power of God flowed through him, spiritual electricity. When this happened, we all heard a thump and knew that God had given the man a brand new heart. He was among those who followed us through the streets. We thought of the words of Jesus:

> *Verily, verily, I say unto you, He that believeth on me, the works that I do shall he do also; and greater works than these shall he do; because I go unto my Father.* John 14:12

As we were doing the works of Jesus, it was no wonder that people followed us as they had followed Him.

We stopped at a little town in the middle of Australia, Roper River. God had told me to go there. When we got off the plane we were greeted by an Aboriginal tribal councilman. He didn't even pretend to know Christ, yet he greeted us warmly and welcomed us to his town.

"We just left your uncle," I told him.

"Oh, how nice," he responded.

Another member of the community greeted us. He turned out to be the local priest, and he quickly made it known that he did not want us there, fearing that we were carriers of false doctrine. We tried to reassure him that we were people of sound doctrine who would only bless his people, but he insisted, "No, you cannot stay here."

The councilman, overhearing this exchange, interrupted, "Yes, you must stay," and we did.

That night we attended a service in the local church, sitting docilely under the ministry of the priest and saying *Amen* to everything he preached. When he saw that we knew the hymns of the church, that we loved the Lord and had a good spirit, he announced at the close of the service, "These people are free to go where they like in the town." To us he said, with pardonable pride, "We have arranged for you to stay with two school teachers." We were grateful because there was no hotel in town.

You might think that two lady school teachers would be just as consecrated as missionaries, but not so in this case. These two were the town party girls. They had issues of *Playboy* on their table. What a shock it must have been when two Holy Ghost preacher ladies were dumped on them! Their daily five o'clock community cocktail hour was totally spoiled.

That afternoon a Jewish boy came to visit. I stood up and with a loud voice prophetically said to him, "It is time to return to Israel." He made some smart remark in response. In the same calm voice, I said, "Well, I'll tell Rabbi G. on you. He wouldn't like to hear that."

When I said that he turned as white as a sheet. "How did you know that Rabbi G. was my spiritual mentor when I was young?" he asked.

"I know him to be a very spiritual man," I answered. "If he could speak with you right now, he would tell you that what I am saying is from God." Soon, his whole life was turned around.

The next day we went down a little path, not knowing exactly where we were going, but we were led of the Spirit. On a porch we saw a black man smoking a pipe. I looked into his eyes and said, "God has called you, and His call is still real."

Tears came into his eyes and he put down the pipe. "It is true," he said. I am backslidden. I know I am supposed to preach." That day he gave his heart back to God and is still preaching the Gospel.

On the way home from another such trip to Australia, we were preaching in a little town on the coast in the church of an Aboriginal pastor. When he saw the miracles God was doing, he asked us to go and pray for a man named Rex Capeen of Cabbage Tree Island. "His mother is a faithful member of our church," he told us. "She is now in her eighties and she has prayed for many years for her unsaved son who was shot in the spinal chord, and is now confined to a wheelchair."

We went and got the mother and took her with us. I only had ten or fifteen minutes to spend with the man, but I pleaded with God: "You must do this, or it won't be done."

When we arrived at the man's house, he sat defiantly smoking a cigarette. "Rex Capeen," I said, "I have come in the name of Jesus Christ to command you to honor

your mother and to honor Christ. Put down that cigarette. You are killing yourself." He did just that, being
shocked into it.

"Now, in the name of Jesus, receive Him as your Lord
and Savior. Ask Him to forgive your sins."

The man bowed his head and wept; and, in that moment, he received Jesus as his Lord and Savior. I laid my
hands on his head and said, "Receive the Holy Ghost and
be healed, in the name of Jesus Christ." Immediately he
began speaking in tongues; and, at the same time he began speaking in tongues, his body began to move. He
gripped the handles of his wheelchair, his whole body
trembling, and stood up, his spinal chord restored by the
power of Almighty God! He stood up for the first time in
years, weeping and speaking in tongues. We all rejoiced
and praised God.

The next year I received a letter from another pastor. It
contained a photograph of Rex Capeen standing with his
arm around his mother. He said that Rex walks around
Cabbage Tree Island, pushing his wheelchair and telling
people what God did for him.

On another occasion, I was in one of the large Aboriginal settlements on the east coast near Lismore. I was
alone this time, and there were two pastors in the settlement. I heard they were having some sort of problem, so I
went to talk to one of them. "The other pastor has lost his
mind," he told me. "He sits in a closed room for hours at a
time and refuses to talk with anyone. The church is suffering because he has become so selfish that he won't let
anyone preach, and he has gone into false doctrine."

"Take me to that pastor," I said. It was nine o'clock at
night, and everyone was already in bed; but as we moved
though the streets, the pastor cried, "The preacher's coming. Everyone up." Soon, people had lined up in their

pajamas and nightgowns to receive ministry. Prophecy came forth. People were slain in their homes in the Spirit.

We finally worked our way down to a house full of rebellious teenagers. Their parents weren't home. We prayed for them, and they wept their way back to God. At last, we arrived at the home of the pastor in question. Time was running out. I had only a few more minutes to stay. We entered the house to find that the man was locked in the bathroom and would not come out. For the first time in my life, I prophesied through a locked bathroom door. The Lord told the man to open his heart, to seek Him, to fast and pray and to give the people, for a time, into the hands of the man sent to help him, and that when he had recovered, he was to lead his people, not to place them into bondage. We later learned that there had been a great shake up in that place and that it had resulted in revival.

On one occasion, the Lord sent me to Alice Springs. I went, not knowing exactly what I was to do there. I stayed in a hotel that first night. In the morning the Lord told me to go visit a well-known, half-aboriginal political leader, and gave me a message for him. I found his office in the center of town. "I want to see your boss," I said to the receptionist.

"I'm sorry," she replied. "He is not in at the moment, and he probably won't be in this morning." Since God had told me to come, I said that I would wait, and I began to pray in the Spirit. While I was waiting, an old man with a dog came in. He also wanted to see the man, so he sat down in the waiting room. He looked at me in a strange way. He didn't know what he was feeling, but he knew he was feeling something.

He looked at me and began to sing the chorus of that old hymn:

At the cross, at the cross where I first saw the light
And the burdens of my heart rolled away.

How wonderful is the power of God! It caused us to have a revival right there in that office.

After a while, the politician and his wife arrived. Before he went into his office, he paused and asked, "Did you want to see me?" He looked at me very strangely and said, "You have a message for me, don't you?"

"Yes, I do," I assured him. I proceeded to introduce myself and to explain who I was, but little time was lost before we got to God's message for him in prophecy. As God began to speak, I looked at the man. He was a liberal and had been called a "Red Ragger" by many, but now he bowed his head in reverence to the Lord of Glory.

He had heard about God from others, the Lord said, but now God was calling him to come and know Him personally. He was to stop worrying about the "hypocrites" who had witnessed to him in the past and to come face to face in a personal meeting with his Maker. "Your desire is to be a leader of the people," the Lord said, "but to do that you must yield yourself to Me, for I am The Leader of the people. Only those whom I approve will lead. Humble yourself before Me and give Me your heart, for I want to make you the leader of your people. There are many people you must forgive; but, first of all, you must allow Me to forgive you."

The next day his wife came to the airport. She was very gracious and thanked me for coming. She knew, she said, that what I said was a message from God. I have often thought about the man and prayed for him that he would permit God to make him the leader he was destined to be. I never saw him again, but I know that God loves him and is very interested in his life.

The whole of Australia is dear to God's heart. Great human dramas have been played out on that "Land Down Under," and in the near future, the orientals will come down and occupy at least the top half of the country. God's prophets have foreseen it. God is sending revival now to prepare His people. He has greater things in store for Australia.

Chapter 8

Morocco

*He delivereth me from mine enemies: yea, thou
liftest me up above those that rise up against me:
thou hast delivered me from the violent man.*

Psalm 18:48

In 1983, after a crusade in Freetown, Sierra Leone, in
West Africa, a group of us stopped overnight in
Casablanca, Morocco on the way home. As we came
through the airport, the Lord said to me, "You will return
in March." It was now December. I turned to Brother
Heflin and told him what the Lord had said.

"Good," he said, "take Sister Jane with you."

After I got home, Jane and I prayed and began making
plans to return to Morocco. There were several complica-
tions: the government of Morocco did not want missions
in their country; they would not permit Bibles or scripture portions of any kind to be handed out; and they
would not permit hiring a hall for a public meeting. We
had the surety that God was going to use us in that

Islamic state and show us how to minister to the Moslem people.

When we landed in Casablanca, we found and purchased a good travel book about the country. It contained a complete list of hotels and a good map of the country. We secured a room which cost us only US $7 a night, and it was one of the best hotels in town. It was clean and well-run.

We immediately fell in love with Morocco. The King of Morocco is a marvelous man. Both he and his father, Mohammed V, have found favor with God by protecting the Moroccan Jews. Synagogues are permitted to operate freely, and the Jewish people are permitted to have their own businesses and to operate without fear. The Moroccans have taken a public stand, in the face of great opposition from the outside, and said, "Leave the Moroccan Jews alone. Don't touch them. They are Moroccans and will be cared for and respected as Moroccans." God honors that stand.

We waited on the Lord in our hotel room, and He spoke to us. He showed us that we should respect the laws of Morocco, that we were not to organize public meetings, that we were not to hand out any Christian literature, that we were to be careful in what we said. "I will cause you to speak My name," He said, "You will heal the sick and leave a testimony in this place; for I am about to move in revival."

The Lord showed us a route for our trip. We started in Casablanca, then we went to Marrakesh, through Zagora and Ourzazate and out into the desert as far as anyone could go by law. We bought Moroccan robes and slippers, dressed ourselves with a scarf tied around our heads, and as the Lord directed us, we went out to the streets, from eight in the morning till eight at night. There we met and ministered to the people.

One of the fruitful areas was the marketplace. Looking for something to buy there became very important to our plan. As we walked from stall to stall and looked for the items we wanted to buy, we began speaking with the people and teaching them individually. Some of the people could not speak English. If not, they usually spoke French. I had studied French rigorously for four years in high school, and it all came back to me now very quickly and, at the end of a week, I was speaking French as if the years in between my studies and my practical use of the language had vanished.

Oh, I made a few mistakes. One day I got a horse meat lung sandwich instead of the horse meat heart sandwich I had ordered. Jane refused my kind offer to share it.

"I know you are a holy person," a merchant would say to me. "Please pray for my wife who is very sick." When we prayed, she was healed. The next time we came by they would have someone else to pray for, perhaps a child. We walked in a glory cloud of His presence, and the people felt it.

They had many questions, and we were able to answer from the Word of God.

When we had finished our time in Casablanca, we boarded a train for Marrakesh. The train was clean and comfortable, a wonderful way to get around the country. We stayed at the Arab equivalent of the YMCA. It was beautiful and looked very much like a palace, yet the cost was only US $4 a night. As we moved further and further into the countryside, toward the desert, the price of the hotels declined even further. One place cost us only US $1.72 per night.

In Marrakesh the Lord spoke to us, "I have brought

you here because I could make you as harmless as doves, but be wise and listen to Me when you answer the questions of the people. In every place into which I will lead you, there will be hungry people. I will bring all the hungry ones to you." It was true. Even on the train we met the hungry ones.

Because it was difficult to lay hands publicly on the people, we would just take their hands in ours, believing God to work through that contact; and as we did, we could feel the power of God flowing from us into them. In this way, for twelve hours a day, and for thirty days, we ministered the fullness of the Lord as we traveled though the towns of Morocco.

Toward the end of our time, we approached one merchant in the marketplace and bought a few things from him to take home. I took his hand and said, "Let me pray for the success of your business."

"Please do," he said.

While I prayed, I spoke to him in a word of knowledge, "The Lord Jesus shows me that your lungs are sick and that He is coming to heal you right now."

His body shook and he said loudly, "I know that God has healed me." Many of his Muslim friends, in their robes and beards, came from every direction to see what was happening.

The Lord had told us the night before in our hotel room, "There will be trouble tomorrow, but speak for Me and I will deliver you."

These men seemed to sense that we were Christians and began shouting very angrily, "God has no wife, and God has no son."

"Just a minute," I said in a loud, commanding voice. "Listen! It is written, 'The Lord your God, He is one God.' " They looked at each other very quizzically. They were puzzled. The anointing of the Holy Ghost had confused them, and they couldn't disagree with that doctrine, so they all went home to lunch and left us alone.

The Lord told us to go up to Rabat and prophesy to the four winds. I noticed on the map a big archway that was called *The Gate of the Four Winds*. We stood in that gate, faced each direction, and prophesied revival into the towns of Morocco.

In each of the larger towns we visited, there was a palace for the king's use. We wept before each of these palaces and prophesied revival and salvation to the king and his family, to the town in which the palace was located, and into all the surrounding territories.

We met only two missionaries while we were in Morocco. We laid hands on one of them, and he was filled with the Holy Ghost.

As we left Morocco, we were aware that we had only seen the tip of the iceberg of victory, but we sensed in our spirits that God had indeed done a great work. We had moved by the Spirit of God and been at just the right place at the right time. The Lord spoke to us as we departed, "The heart of the king is in My hand. I will turn it whithersoever I will."

In the ensuing years, I often thought of what God did in Morocco. God has a special way of evangelizing, in the Spirit, every place on the Earth. In Morocco, He used women because they seemed harmless to the powers that be. They did not require great advertising campaigns. They were not concerned if their names were not written in lights. They didn't care if anyone ever knew they had been there (except the devil and the angels and the people they had ministered to). The spirits of Islam are male oriented and believe that women can do nothing, and women blend in with the people so that they could minister to them.

Islam is very widespread. The Oriental people have Moslems among them. The African Christians have trouble with Moslems in many of their countries. Since our ministry in Morocco, I have contended that there is a right way and a wrong way to minister to Moslems. Anyone who is willing to go in God's way, making themselves of no reputation, going in low-keyed, but with power and without fear, they can reap a harvest for the Lord. God is moving sovereignly among the Islamic nations of the world.

No place is closed to the Gospel, no place is impossible to evangelize, no place is so dangerous that the Spirit of God cannot make a way to bless those who hunger for Him. Of every nation, kindred, tribe and tongue, God Almighty will have a people.

Chapter 9

Mexico

*For thou wilt save the afflicted people; but wilt bring
down high looks.*   Psalm 18:27

About eight years ago I felt led to pray all night for two
nights in a row. The Lord told me He had some special
things He wanted me to do, but that I would have to
make a more serious dedication to Him and get closer to
Him if I expected to do these things. I am convinced that
God has great works for each of us to do, if we will only
seek His face and be willing to invest our lives in His
purposes.

We often sing that chorus:

> *I'll go where You want me to go, dear Lord*
> *O'er mountain or plain or sea.*
> *I'll say what You want me to say, dear Lord.*
> *I'll be what you want me to be.*

But are we really His? Unless He speaks to us of someplace well-known or big or important, we are usually

slow to hear His voice. Who will go to the out-of-the-way places to do the bidding of the Lord?

When the Lord began to speak to Isaiah and show him His missionary heart, the prophet responded with that lovely phrase, *"Here am I"* (Isaiah 6:8). I was determined to do the same.

There was a lady missionary visiting the camp who had once been a nun, a very gentle and precious soul who had much love for God. I asked her to join me in prayer. We determined to keep each other awake so that we could receive something new from the Lord.

We walked back and forth in my living room and dining room praying out loud in English. Then we would pray a while in tongues. We would worship a while. Then we would wait upon the Lord and walk in His presence.

One the second night of prayer, God spoke to me. He reminded me that my dear friend Debbie Kendrick had just come back from a place in Yucatan where He had sent her. "I have more work to be done there," He told me now, "and I want you to go. Go to the Yucatan Peninsula. I want you to go to Cancun and Cozumel, and I also have places in the interior where you must speak."

I knew that the Yucatan Peninsula was that part of Mexico that sticks out into the Caribbean Sea. I sensed that I would be visiting three or four Indian churches there and that God was preparing me through much prayer because there would be no translator. Although my Spanish was not as good as it should be for fired-up preaching, it would have to do.

Who should I take with me? I have always believed that women going forth should go two by two, so I had to look for another woman to accompany me. Of the many wonderful lady missionaries of the camp, most either had

other important things to do or were already out somewhere preaching. As I prayed, I felt that the perfect
companion for me on this trip was not someone from the
camp. Then I saw a vision of Sister Sally Lessing of Ft.
Wayne, Indiana. She and her husband had accompanied
us on many successful mission trips, notably into Russia
and the Holy Land. Richard Lessing, in fact, had helped
us on some very dangerous missions. I knew Sister Sally
to be a good wife and a good mother, a woman who had
brought up her own family well and kept her life pure.

I called Richard and told him about the vision I had
received. "I have been asking God for two days to show
me who to take with me on my trip to Mexico," I explained.

When I said that, he let out a whoop. "You will not
believe this," he said. "Some weeks ago, I had a dream in
which I saw my wife and myself taking treasures out of
Mayan temples."

"That is exactly the area we are going to," I assured
him. "We will be going into the interior of the Yucatan
Peninsula. The descendants of the Mayas still live there.
There are many Mayan ruins in the area."

Richard was very pleased and told his wife what we
were talking about. She was very happy to accompany
me, and within a week we were on our way, having sent a
telegram in Spanish to the pastors of the churches in
Cancun and Cozumel, telling them that we would be
coming for a two-week stay.

In the air, just before we arrived in Cancun, I had a
sense of the demon activity over that place, and I was
determined to go in with victory and to take authority
over them. We let every enemy of God know that we
were coming with His power and that revival was surely
here.

The pastor had sent some of his members to receive us.
We spoke in the church for several days with wonderful
results. God healed many and filled many with the Holy
Ghost, and many people rededicated their lives to the
Lord.

We went to one of the islands for a week of ministry.
Many miracles were done. The church was starting a
building program, and God used us to build their faith.
He spoke to us to leave a sizable gift as well.

One night we visited a church where the pastor was
said to be living in sin. God used us to speak His Word
with power and authority, and many people were delivered from Satan's power.

In the final days of our visit we preached in the interior,
in very primitive places. One of the churches had no roof
as yet. The pastor had struggled to establish a work in
that place while some of the local people were so opposed to his work that they continually threatened to kill
him. We stood nightly under the unfinished structure
and preached, and God moved mightily upon the people
of that place. Each night, however, while we preached, an
angry and threatening crowd gathered out front.

Then God did an unusual thing: I have rarely been sick
on my mission journeys, but this time I became very ill, so
ill that I felt I had to sleep outside the house that night
(there was no indoor plumbing). I would take advantage
of the time to pray for the persecutors. There were no
extra beds in the house, as it turned out, and no extra
hammocks, and since I didn't want the pastor and his
wife to give up their hammocks for me, I made myself
comfortable on two chairs, as comfortable as I could be
because I was violently sick all night. Between bouts of
nausea, however, I was calling on Jesus and speaking in

tongues, interceding for those who were opposing the Gospel in that place.

Toward morning, a wonderful miracle took place. Actually, two wonderful miracles took place. I was healed, and the angry crowd dispersed. I have often felt that my illness had the purpose of maintaining me awake and prayerful during that time to intercede for the people of that place, and when Satan saw that we would not be moved and that we were determined to stay and minister to the people, he let us alone.

Back in Cancun, we had a special mission to perform. Being on the Board of Trustees of Calvary Pentecostal Tabernacle has required that I have much faith. We have done a lot of building through the years, and I have had to both have faith for that building and a knowledge of building terms and building plans. As the pastor of the church spread his building plans before me, I was able to exercise faith for his project. When we left we had the assurance that their faith had come alive and that what God had told them He was going to do would surely come to pass. They were not to look to the bank, nor to look to the contribution that others would make, but to look to God. We left the people revived and on-fire for God, with a new zeal for holiness and a new faith for God's provision.

That final week in Yucatan I celebrated my birthday in a tiny hotel room which the church in Cancun had reserved for us. Very late that night I heard the strains of guitars outside our window. All the people of the church had gathered to serenade me on my birthday. They also gave me one of the finest gifts I have ever received, a cotton dress with colorful floral designs, just like the dresses they wear themselves. I thank God for the privilege of taking His Word to the far reaches of the Earth and that I could stand with Him for revival.

Again, what we saw happening with our eyes in the Yucatan Peninsula was just the tip of the iceberg. Until we see Jesus, no one will ever know how many lives were changed in that place in a very short time. Many prophecies went forth, and only eternity will reveal the harvest we reaped. So, even if we don't know the language very perfectly, when God calls, we can obey. He gives the message; He changes the lives of men; and every victory is His.

Chapter 10

Nepal

The strangers shall fade away, and be afraid out of their close places.   Psalm 18:45

Some years ago, during a trip to China, Brother Heflin was talking to Brother Charles Mendies, a young Nepali Christian leader, about a forthcoming teaching session that Charles felt led to have in a far village of Nepal, his home at that time. The village was many days' journey from the capital city, Katmandu. He and his people had evangelized a village some time before, but when Hindus saw what was happening, they were very angry and forced those who had believed in Jesus to leave the village. This resulted in the Christians having a village of their own further down the road. They were, thus, able to continue their meetings without too much interference, and, as always happens, the Christian village prospered more than those around it. Having been ordered out of their persecutors' village proved to be a good thing. It enabled the people who had been converted to go on for the Lord in a greater way.

It was announced, therefore, that Brother Heflin had been invited to do some teaching of the workers in Nepal. He would have to leave in January (also wintertime in Nepal) and go into the southern valleys of that country. The villages there, we were told, do not experience the cold that strikes Katmandu, for they are protected by the mountains. What we were not told was that there were a series of high mountains and six rivers that had to be crossed to reach those villages.

Because Brother Heflin was invited, and because it was a difficult place to reach, it was logical that none of us women could go along but, for some reason, I began to get a burden to go and minister to those primitive people (a special love of my heart in many places in the world). I began to pray for Nepal. Then, a strange thing happened: As Charles began to prophesy over Brother Heflin (we were all crowded around them), I began jumping up and down with excitement over the idea of going to Nepal for the Lord and, with my eyes closed, I inadvertently jumped between the one giving the prophecy and the one receiving it.

With the many activities of the tour to China, we soon forgot about the matter — until about a week after we got home. Then, one morning Brother Heflin came down and announced to our office staff that God had spoken to him the evening before that he was to stay home, and that instead of him going to Nepal, he was sending me. Although this was the first time I had heard from him that I was to go, I had already felt it in the Spirit. I was thrilled.

I needed a companion and began to pray about that. As I prayed, I saw the face of one of our lady preachers, Dora Sites, the wife of Paul Sites, the pastor of our West Point Church for many years. Dora was a good homemaker, a good mother, and a good pastor's wife; and I knew that she would be an excellent missionary. She is a surrendered and dedicated woman who preaches and lives a life of holiness. I thanked the Lord for His choice. When I called her and told her what the Lord had showed me, she was happy to accept, and we made our travel plans.

An American pastor from Illinois and a Nepali team were also invited. When we arrived in Nepal late at night, we were taken to Mendies Haven, the famous children's home founded by Charles' parents and later run by him and his wife Susan. The children are given a Christian home, so fine that the King of Nepal has recommended children to them. It has a lovely, clean atmosphere.

It was damp and cold in Katmandu, and we had to use a lot of blankets to keep warm during the night. Just before we went to bed, Charles said to me, "You ladies will need your rest. Tomorrow we must cross six rivers." I wondered what was so difficult about crossing six rivers. Then suddenly it dawned on me.

"Charles," I said knowingly, "Tell me. There are no boats, are there?"

Charles smiled broadly and replied, "No. You're right, Sister Weidemann. There are no boats." And with that we retired for the night.

Before I slept I pondered what it meant to cross six rivers in Nepal without boats. I learned that it meant warm underclothing, an old *sari* borrowed from the cook (since the water of those mountain streams is noted for two things: being ice cold and being loaded with silt). What I wore through those six rivers I would not be wearing again. As I drifted off into sleep, I dedicated myself for whatever lie ahead.

In the morning, a large group of Nepalis had assembled to accompany us, preachers and their wives, carriers, for the many bundles of clothing and Bibles we would take to the people, and cooks. Dora and I rose early and prepared a small bag that we would take along for the trip. The bags contained our Bibles and a change of clothing. We simply had to travel light. These bags would have to be carried through six rivers and up and down many mountains on either side of those rivers.

Charles had an old bus that we packed ourselves into for the first part of the journey. We drove nearly all day until we came to a small village, where we stopped for the night. We slept on small cots in the loft of one of the local houses. The next morning we had a breakfast of rice and then boarded the bus again for our trip to the first river, where we disembarked on the river bank.

We thought that we were ready to do anything for the Lord, that our consecration would take us anywhere, but as we stepped off that bus and realized that we would be on foot for the next ten days or two weeks and looked across that bubbling river, we knew that this would not be an ordinary missionary trip.

We were not yet down far enough to have escaped the bitter cold and, as we stepped into that first river and the ice cold water crept up until our thighs felt like frozen turkeys, we had to be physically pulled across to the other side, wet to our shoulders.

We were not walking on a sandy bottom or even the common pebbles. The bottom was covered with boulders the size of basketballs, and they were covered with slippery moss and mud. I had wondered why the Lord had told me, before I left home to take some sturdy boots. I was so glad now that I had obeyed. There was no way that my tender feet could have survived the days of walking through rocky river bottoms.

The current was swift in some places, and we were covered in icy water up to our necks. In one river, there was only one narrow sand bar on which we could cross through the water. Without the help of the Nepalis our lives would have been in grave danger, for we could have very easily fallen into a large hole on either side and been swept away by the current.

The flowing *saris* were a special hindrance when crossing the rivers, but we had determined long ago not to disobey the Lord by wearing pants. We believed that God was able to protect us and that if we obeyed Him we would be spared from hardships we might encounter otherwise.

Jesus said:

> *Behold, I give unto you power to tread on serpents*
> *and scorpions, and over all the power of the enemy:*
> *and nothing shall by any means hurt you.*
>
> Luke 10:19

Only obeying God brings joy and victory.

We slogged onward, learning very early to bend down, when we were in the water, to pick up the bottom of the skirt of the *sari* and hold it out of the way of our feet so that we could walk through with greater ease. Our progress was very slow, and, as we climbed out of each river bank and stood on dry boulders beside the river, we looked straight up to yet another steep mountain. The river valleys seemed to be in wilderness canyons made of stone. The mountains that loomed ahead would prove to have inclines of forty-five degrees and sometimes up to sixty degrees, and going down proved every much as difficult as going up. Sometimes we found ourselves sliding down the granite face of the rock. As we went cautiously down these steep places, I wondered how we would get back up them on the return trip.

When we got across each river, I had to empty my boots so that I could go on. Thankfully we never got our long hair wet because it would have taken too long to dry in that cold.

We experienced physical weariness because of the rugged terrain we were traversing. We slipped wearily at night into strange huts and way stations, where we were greeted with a cup of hot tea, a plate of rice, and a cotton mat to be spread on the ground for sleep.

When we reached those valleys, so far from home, so far from family and friends, so far from any American embassy and its legal and moral help, I got a new vision of the joy of trusting God completely for one's safety and sustenance. I knew, however, that at the end of the trail, we would be satisfied by a complete ministry to hungry people. After several days of seemingly endless travel, we reached our destination, where we were received by the local headmen and the villagers.

Sister Sites and I were placed in a small, upstairs loft made of saplings stripped of their bark. It was in a farmhouse, between a mountain and a rice paddy on the edge of the river. There were no bathrooms, no showers and no electricity. When you wanted a drink, boiled tea was the only choice. When it was mealtime, you received a tin pie plate filled with rice with vegetable soup over it, and occasionally a chicken stew.

We began to teach the people, and our pulpits were haystacks. The workers of the village, hungry to hear of the moving of God, of the ways of God, and of the Word of God, and to see the power of God in demonstration, would gather around us. After the classes, we would lay hands on the people and pray for the sick and prophesy over them. In this way, the workers saw the practical application of the Word.

At night we gathered around the campfire and sang and preached and taught and had Holy Ghost services, which themselves are the best teacher, for it is the Living Word for which the people hunger. In such a service people not only hear, they feel and experience God.

When the people of other villages heard the singing and rejoicing and knew of the healing miracles, they came bringing their sick, and many were saved. Toward the end of our stay, we held a baptismal service in the river for those who wanted to make a full commitment to their new life in the Lord. At the conclusion of that service a man ran up and whispered in Charles' ear. He turned to me and said, with a serious demeanor, "Sister Weidemann, in the morning, the Hindu police will come for us."

We had known before we went there that it was dangerous to preach the Gospel in Nepal and to baptize converts. Charles would later spend months in prison for doing so.

We had another meeting that night, and we prayed and prophesied as before, without fear. There was a very important old man nearby, a Hindu, and he had received us several times in his hut for dinner, but he was evidently displeased with something we had done and had reported us to the authorities.

We went to sleep that night, but the Nepali believers stayed up all night singing and praying in the Spirit, fully expecting trouble the next day and concerned with protecting those of us who had come. It was very touching to hear their songs in the night and to know that they were watching over us. We slept soundly.

In the morning Charles said that word had come that the police were on their way with rifles and machine guns. He had determined not to have a confrontation.

"We will surrender to them when we meet them on the road," he said. "If we don't give ourselves up, they will torture the villagers to find out where we are."

My spirit refused to surrender to Hindu persecution or to recognize the authority of those who were coming to lay hold on us, so I said, "Charles, we will do what we must do. We'll trust the Lord."

We gave our last blessings and started down the road, twenty-seven of us, the bearers coming behind. We made our way down a narrow dirt path. There were no cars, no telephone poles, no electrical wires, no post offices, no stores, no way stations. This was the wilderness of Nepal, and we seemed to be alone there. At every bend in the road, however, we expected to meet those who were sent to take us into custody and place us in a dank Nepali prison, as they had done to so many others before us. Some Christians had been held for as long as six years without trial, and the foreign embassies seemed power-less to prevent it.

Hindu law is very powerful, but between us and all danger stood the blood of Jesus, the power of our God, and the unseen presence of our accompanying angels. We were not afraid. We went on our way worshiping Jesus, some speaking in tongues, while others were sing-ing hymns.

In the Indian and Nepali churches, the *sari* worn over the woman's head is a symbol of her subjection to man. Now, I removed the *sari* from my head, and I lifted my face to Heaven and said, "Lord, show everybody how You protect Your widows. I trust You. You called us here to teach. We came without fear, and we return without fear, for You are with us. We are all safe under Your protection." As we made our way along that ox path, I sang that old hymn *When the Roll Is Called Up Yonder*.

The sun beat down on us and was soon scorching the white skin of those of us who were Americans. I held my hands up over my head to protect my face, but I could only keep them there so long. Then, I looked up and said, "Lord Jesus, shield us from this heat." Immediately clouds formed and covered the sun, and a soft haze filled the air. It felt to us like the glory cloud we had sometimes experienced in our meetings.

As the minutes turned into hours and still we had not met anyone on the path, we felt relieved and began praising the Lord even more. We sensed, at last, that we were on our way home. We kept moving along the path, walking in single file with perhaps twenty feet between us. Suddenly, there was a commotion. Someone was running, and there was an excited flurry at the head of our column.

Charles called back to me, "Sister Weidemann, did you see that? Did you hear?"

"What, Charles?" I asked.

"This man was at the end of the line," he said. "He just came running to say that he saw five armed Hindu policemen pass our group. These must be the men who were coming to arrest us. The Lord has done a great miracle and blinded their eyes. They did not see us."

It had to be double miracle, I quickly realized, for God had blinded our eyes as well. We were intent on giving ourselves up to the police to prevent the suffering of the Christian villagers, but we had not seen the policemen, and they had not seen us. Only God can do such a miracle. How we rejoiced that day!

When we arrived at the river, we noticed that the current was even swifter than when we had crossed the last time. We got through the first river and up another mountain and down the other side (sliding half way). My *sari* was getting tattered, but I didn't care. Katmandu was getting closer with every step.

We went on, through another river and up another mountain and down and through and up. When we got to the next river, we realized that fully four hours had been shaved off the time it took us to cover the same territory when we went in. God had performed a miracle for a very tired group of His people, but the greatest danger lay just ahead. This was the river with the narrow sand bar on which we must all cross, the sand bar with deep holes on each side, and it was growing quite dark by now. We sensed the guiding and protecting presence of the Lord, and all of us passed safely though the water that night. It was only later that we were told that poisonous snakes roam the surface of the river at night!

As we emerged on the other bank of the ice-cold river, in complete darkness (it was by now nine o'clock at night), we had aching muscles and weary bodies but happy hearts. We were anxious to get to a nearby village to rest for the night. We could see the glimmer of the lamps up ahead. It looked so close. As it turned out, it wasn't close at all. We were fooled by the clear night air. The lamps were two miles away, and we would reach the village only after another good hike. We were soaking wet and the air was cold.

Along the banks of this river were fervent Hindu pilgrims in several encampments. We would have to enter the village with them on each side of us. Would they try to stop us? We could hear their heathen chants as we approached and moved closer to them. By the same grace of God (our glory cloud) with which we had evaded the policemen, we passed between the enemy camps and safely reached the village. Oh the joy and satisfaction of work well done, of seeing God's Word prevail, the victory always won!

When we arrived at our resting place that night, we stumbled across the threshold, bone weary. I was too tired to reach out for my cup of hot tea. One of the kind Nepalis brought it to me shortly before I fell asleep. It seemed like only moments before we were awakened. It was feared that the Hindu police would seek us out. We needed to move on and travel under cover of night. We boarded the bus that would take us back to Katmandu. Swaying like a cradle for its tired and sleepy passengers, it carried us the eight hours to the capital. The floor of the bus was very dirty and hot from the engine, but it didn't matter. I got down and lay on the floor. My pillow was the baggage of the workers, but I slept.

There is a joyful finish to this story. A year later Charles Mendies came to visit our church in America. Driving home in the car that night, he said to me, "Sister Weidemann, do you remember the headman of the village who invited us to his house several times? They called him 'an important man,' but he was a Hindu witch doctor. He gave us three heavily poisoned meals and expected all of us to drop dead. Every day he watched us, amazed that we carried on as before. He couldn't believe it when I returned to the village later. When he saw me, he cried out with a loud voice, 'These people have more power than I do.' Some months later, he delivered his heart to Jesus." How we rejoiced for such a notable miracle. Poison cannot kill us. We felt no pain in our stomachs.

Jesus promised:

> *And these signs shall follow them that believe; In my name shall they cast out devils; they shall speak with*

new tongues; They shall take up serpents; and if they
drink any deadly thing, it shall not hurt them; they
shall lay hands on the sick, and they shall recover.

Mark 16:17-18

His Word is true. We have proved Him over and over
again.

Chapter 11

Ecuador and Brazil Revisited

Thou hast delivered me from the strivings of the people; and thou hast made me the head of the heathen: a people whom I have not known shall serve me. Psalm 18:43

Because Jesus is coming soon, there is a winding-up of loose ends in the lives and ministries of God's people everywhere. When you have ministered in a place and there has been a foundation laid, as in Brazil twenty years ago, and in Ecuador sixteen years ago, there comes another wave, so to speak.

God spoke to me about going back to Ecuador, so I went with a group of ministers led by Brother Harold McDougal. There we had wonderful opportunities to minister to the church in Quito, to the students in the Bible school and to the outlying congregations. This latter ministry is always my special joy. Many ministers go to the capital cities of the world. Few, however, are willing to go out into the lesser populated and, thus, more primitive areas. I am always looking for the ministers who

have come to the conferences from far places and would
like for someone to go back with them and minister to
their people.

In Ecuador, I have fallen in love with the Quechua
speaking Indians, especially the Otavalo Indians who live
about two hundred miles north of the capital in the high
Andes Mountains. What a noble tribe! The *Otavaleños* are
among the finest weavers in the world and their woolen
goods — ponchos, sweaters and blankets especially —
are sold by them all over the world. I have seen them in
Moscow, Amsterdam and New York.

I was privileged to visit and minister to them first sixteen years ago. While I was visiting their town, the Lord
told me to stay there for six weeks. I had only a small bag
with me, but I rented a small room and settled down
there. Sister Diane McDougal (who's husband was then
the director of the training center in Quito), sent up two
young men (Wilson Aguayo and Gustavo Carerra) to
help me. I could hold my own in a normal conversation,
but I preferred a translator for the preaching to make sure
I said every word correctly. I gave the two brothers my
rented room and moved in with a family from the local
church.

The young men brought along a very useful portable
microphone, so we were able to preach in the streets. We
stopped on a street corner, and the young men began to
sing over the microphone until a little crowd of people
gathered. Then we preached to them.

"We're Catholic here!" shouted one large Indian, "And
we don't want to change."

The Holy Ghost came upon me, and I said, "Change
your heart, not your religion." Then the Lord caused me
to add, "The Pope is Catholic, and he's not a drunkard."

With that, the man slunk away to the edge of the crowd to listen.

Of the sixty people who gathered that day, most of them indicated a desire to accept the Lord as their Savior. Aside from the street meetings, we went house to house, meeting people and ministering to their spiritual needs. We preached in the prison. Eight or nine hardened criminals surrendered their hearts to Jesus. Those were glorious days!

My main mission was unusual: The Lord had given me a dream while I was still at the camp outside of Quito. I had seen the Otavalo men (with their long pigtails, and dressed in their white pedal pushers, their black velveteen slippers, their fedora hats and their beautiful ponchos) receiving Jewish people who were in danger in the last days and needed to hide from authorities and be transported from one country to another. I saw the Otavalans dressing these Jewish people to look like themselves, even going so far as to put false pigtails on them and, in this way, transporting them from one country to another safely. (The Otavalans travel widely for commerce with their unique products.) The Lord had said to me, "You must give them a burden for My people, Israel." That had been my original goal in going to Otavalo.

As I tried to reach out to the leaders in the Otavalo Christian community, I found that they were, for the most part, under the influence of a lady missionary connected with a large denomination, a denomination that no longer believed in the baptism of the Holy Ghost. I approached the woman, but I found her to be very antagonistic toward Pentecostals. In fact, she refused to allow me to speak to their local congregation. As I left her place of business, I walked through the town square weeping, crying out to God, "Lord, You sent me here, and these are Your people. You must help me to speak to them." At that very moment, one of the elders of the people approached me and began a conversation. Before long, I had told him everything that was on my heart.

"Where are you speaking?" he asked.

I told him, and that night he and several more of the local men came to the place I was preaching. I laid hands on them and gave them instructions about God's end-time plan for the Jewish people. The last time I visited them, I found that many Jewish people have purchased land in the area and have greenhouses that can be seen along the major highways.

Because of their hard working ethic, many of the Otavalans are prosperous and have fine vehicles and television sets. That week I was amazed to see on television the story of the holocaust. I was confidant that many of them had seen it, too. God had given me a lot of help with the people.

Although her husband had been a believer at one time, the woman I rented the room from was very hardened to the Gospel. I spoke to her about the Lord, but she would not receive my words. I prayed and wept much for her soul that week. The second week I moved to the home of one of the deacons and moved the two young translators into that rented room. At the end of the second week, a terrible tragedy occurred. The woman came to me sobbing, threw her arms around me and told me how her young grandson, whom she loved dearly, had just been run over by a truck. His head was crushed, and he died instantly. This great tragedy was used to soften the woman's heart, and she gave her life to the Lord Jesus before the week had ended.

While I was in Otavalo, the deacon and his wife with whom I was staying began to tell me about a little Pentecostal church in a village that sat atop a mountain like a little crown, a place called Selva Alegre. It was many hours away from Otavalo and very hard to get to, by bus and by foot. This man felt a burden for the place and God told him in the middle of the night that I was to go there and preach. When he told me, I said that I would pray about it and see what the Lord had to say. Sometimes the Lord speaks to us through others, and we must be humble enough to accept that fact and obey. We must be able to hear His voice in many ways. That night I received nothing from the Lord but the sense that I should honor the man's leading and go.

The next morning I told him that I was willing. If we were going, we had to go quickly because the trip would take time. By this time another translator had arrived from Quito, an American, Kepler Nigh. So the four of us, Brother Kepler and his wife and the deacon and I set off in a jouncing, noisy bus on an eight-hour trip through the winding mountain roads. The noise was generated by a tape player, turned up to full volume. The driver was playing the worldly music of the area. It was nearly deafening.

Before we left, the Lord had told me that the way would be "long and rough," so I was prepared for the worst. I had brought a flight bag with my personal items to Otavalo, but I felt now that I could not even take that. I took only my Bible and what I could get into my purse.

When we came to the end of the road, it was an hour before sunset. Because Ecuador straddles the Equator, every day is twelve hours long, and every night is twelve hours long — during both summer and winter. The only change in the seasons comes when it rains. It would soon be very dark and there was no vehicle to meet us. As we looked off to the mountains ahead of us, the deacon said

that it would take us twelve more hours to reach Selva
Alegre.

It had been raining and the roads were covered with
foot-thick mud. It was on those muddy country roads
that we would make our way toward our final destination. The mud was so bad in places that we could not
walk through it with shoes. It sucked them off our feet.
We had to leave them off.

As the path wound up into the mountains, we grew
short of breath because of the altitude. Even the deacon, a
native, was having a hard time. Halfway up one of the
mountains, he looked at me and said, "Where is this
camp that you have come from? What place trains workers for this? Who teaches you to love our people so much?
I am sure that you live in a nice home, so the fact that you
would come and do this for us is very touching. It
humbles me." And, with that, he began to cry.

We don't realize, many times, that people are watching
our actions very closely when we have preached to them.
Our consecration (or lack of it) shows in the times of diffi-
culty or trial.

What made me go on was not just the training I had
received in the camp. It was the power of the Holy Ghost
in me that caused me to love Jesus enough to be willing to
go anywhere He wanted. He requires this kind of devotion, and I am glad to give it.

As darkness fell, we realized that it would be very difficult for us to go on. Coming upon a military encampment,
we enquired if we could stay there for the night. The
military officials reluctantly told us that it was against
orders to permit any civilians to stay in the barracks, and
we were forced onward in the ever-increasing darkness.

We came upon a pathway that we needed to take and
saw, to our surprise, that there was a large bull coming

up on our left. The translator cried out, "In the name of Jesus, STOP!" The bull seemed to care nothing for the name of Jesus and kept on coming, so we decided to hasten our steps and move on out of his way. In that moment, my shoes came off again. I turned back and looked directly in the face of the bull and said, "In the name of Jesus, I will not preach without my shoes." I plucked the shoes out of the mud and ran on. The bull seemed startled for a moment but then continued to follow us.

Just then, the owner of the bull, a local farmer, appeared. He was very shamefaced and apologized for the actions of his bull. "*El es bravo,*" he told us. (He is an angry bull.) We wholeheartedly agreed and were relieved to see him take control of the bull and turn him aside into his own pasture.

The bull chasing us turned out to be a blessing. The farmer owned a tiny shack nearby. We never knew exactly what the shack was for, but we suspected that it was used as either a still or a storage place for home brew because the man said that if we could wait while he cleared some bottles out of the shack, we could stay there for the night. We gratefully accepted and slept soundly that night in the moonshiner hut on mats on the floor.

He graciously offered us bowls of thick, hot soup and rice. We shared with him some of the money we had and, in the morning, we continued our way up the mountain. The conditions had not changed, and we often had to remove our shoes and walk in deep mud up the hillside. Every now and then we would meet a farmer along the way and ask how far it was to Selva Alegre. The answer was always the same, very hospitable and usually erroneous, "Only ten or fifteen minutes more." It was an hour more just to the next mountain. Finally, we arrived at the last mountain, and the village of Selva Alegre appeared as a little crown on top of it.

The few Christians in the village came out to greet us. Among them was a ten-year-old girl. She came running up to me, put her arms around me and hugged me tightly. I looked down at her and was shocked to discover a hideous cancer growing out from a scar on her neck. "What is this?" I asked those who were with her.

"It's cancer," they told me, "She had one operation already, but now the cancer has returned."

I wept as I laid my hands over that cancer and prayed and cursed that thing. I commanded the cancer to leave. Within two days, the cancer had disappeared.

The church in Selva Alegre was suffering from lack of leadership. Because it was such a far place, none of the pastors from the surrounding communities liked to come there. There was another reason: the church was poor and could not afford to give a pastor bus fare to come. The church had no electricity, and most of the members walked barefooted. The church had also been split with false doctrine. Jesus loved the people of Selva Alegre and had sent us to bless them. Our first task was to spiritually feed the people. Many new believers were added to the church that week in Selva Alegre.

It was said that an important man in the village was living in sin. I felt led to go to him and speak with him about the things of God. I told him about the cleansing power of the blood of Jesus and admonished him to prepare for eternity. He was very humbled by my visit and was pleased to receive Jesus as his Savior. Other couples were saved as well.

Because of the difficult journey, I had brought only the dress I had on. After a few days, it badly needed washing.

One afternoon, I went to bed while the ladies washed my dress.

The elderly couple with which we were housed offered me the only bed in the house. I thanked them, but didn't feel that I should take their bed. "I will be happy here," I told them, patting the uncompromisingly hard boards of a bench in the hall. That is where I stayed, praying that God would preserve my bones as I turned on the "bed" at night.

Those were precious days. I loved the black and white cows that clung to the sides of the mountains and loved the milk I was served with steamed banana and a lump of molasses for breakfast. There was corn in the nearby fields. Some of it was ground for soup and hot drinks, while some was popped and placed on the top of the soup. Live guinea pigs scurried about on the dirt floors of the local kitchens. They are a valuable delicacy for the Ecuadorian highlanders, and a visitor who is offered guinea pig is highly honored. The meat is fried, much as we would fry rabbits, and is very tasty. When my turn came to eat guinea pig, however, I did so with very mixed emotions. I was hungry and the meat was delicious, but guinea pigs were among the many little pets I kept through the years when my children were growing up. I loved them, so I ate them now with an odd sadness. It happened in this rather comical way:

One day, while I was visiting a lady's home, I was petting her guinea pigs. "*Le gusta?*" she asked me. (Do you like it?)

"*Sí, mucho,*" I answered. (Yes, very much.)

I meant one thing, but she meant something entirely different. When it came time for lunch, I found my erstwhile friend, the guinea pig, fried and placed over the rice on my plate.

"Oh," I said rather sadly, "now he'll think that I'm a terrible hypocrite. I played with him this morning, and now I'm eating him for lunch." He was delicious.

When we were teaching in one of the houses at night, other people heard about it and came to fill the house. Many wondrous things were done. Many were healed and many others were filled with the Spirit.

The people of Selva Alegre became, to me, like members of my own family. I love them and will never forget them.

Because there was no electricity, we used kerosene lamps or candles at night. I found it very difficult to read my Bible in that dim light, so I had to give forth the Word of Life out of the fund of reserves laid up inside me through the years. How wonderful to have a loving heavenly Father Who is the Bread of Life! He is meat and milk and wine to all those who hunger and thirst for Him. Our inability to see the pages of the Bible or read it aloud does not hinder Him from feeding His little ones.

One day I was on my way down the side of the mountain to teach the Word of God in someone's house, accompanied by one of the young girls of the village. They followed me wherever I went. God had spoken to me and said, "You had to leave your own daughters at home sometimes to preach my Word. I will give you the love of many daughters," and He was true to His word.

One particular sunny afternoon I was on my way down a muddy path, accompanied by a little girl who carried my shoes and our lunch of bananas, when we came upon what looked to me like a large, transparent or iridescent worm, lying in the mud by the side of the road. I took my bare foot and turned him over. As I did that, the little girl's eyes widened in fear. After we had arrived at the house where we would preach, she shouted in Spanish,

"The missionary played with a poisonous snake." In that moment I realized again that, although we are often ignorant to the dangers that we face along life's way, God's protection is perfect. He knows, and that's enough for me.

That wonderful week had to end, and with great reluctance I took my leave from that place and returned to Otavalo, loaded down with two live chickens in a sack. They were presented to me by the people of the church of Selva Alegre as their love offering. As I turned to wave at them one last time, a woman stood barefooted in the road and said in Spanish, "God guide your way." I wept.

The chickens traveled under my seat on the bus, softly clucking all the way, and I presented them to my hosts in Otavalo. I felt very much a part of the people.

When the day soon came to leave Otavalo as well, I did so feeling great victory. We had taught and preached in the streets, in the marketplace, in the church, in the jail and from house to house. God had done wondrous things. At least seventeen *Otavaleños* had been filled with the Spirit during our stay and had received a burden for the Jewish people.

In Quito, everyone was happy to hear about what God had done among the Indian people, and soon I found myself waving good-bye to the people there and boarding a plane for home, not knowing that it would be many years before I returned.

Now, sixteen years later, one of my deepest desires was to revisit Otavalo. First, however, I was invited by Pastor and Mrs. Miguel Rodriguez to visit their work in Riobamba. I had a wonderful week there, teaching and preaching. Having spent years in administration and leadership, I felt that I had some very special things to share with the pastor himself. Church administration is no small thing. He was hungry for help from Heaven.

The church was filled and, as always, there was a hunger among the people of Riobamba to know more about the gifts of the Spirit and the ways of the Spirit. Many were filled with the Spirit that week. During the day, many people came and sat around our feet on the floor in the pastor's living room, listening to our teachings. I was delighted to see many of the Indian people coming. Their flute music is hauntingly beautiful. I love it. When they are saved and filled with the Holy Ghost, they seem to reach into the heavens with their flutes and bring down glorious, thrilling melodies. Many other instruments are played in the services and the people can go on for hours worshipping the Lord without seeming to tire. Many people were healed and grew deeper in the things of the Lord that week.

Back in the conference in Quito, I stood with the ministers and the students and wept with them and wept over them and delivered to them the messages that God had ordained from Heaven. During our stay, they were visibly raised to new heights in worship and taken to new depths of dedication. As a mother in Israel, that week I asked to stay with the female students in their dorm. If I had wished it, the brothers would have provided me with private quarters, but this was not my desire. I wanted to treat them like "my girls," and they, in turn, treated me like their mother. They just fluttered around me doing anything they could to make my stay more comfortable, and they never tired of hearing instruction in the things of God. What a thrill it is to teach those who genuinely want to learn. I gave them as much as time would allow, staying up until late at night with some of them. When I had to leave at the end of that week, it was like tearing something apart.

I was not about to be satisfied to leave Ecuador without seeing the people of Otavalo one more time. Each time I had gone, I had seen amazing spiritual progress among the people, and I was very excited to return now for three wonderful days.

There was no interpreter available, so I went alone, catching one of the new minivans that ply the route between Otavalo and the capital. The indigenous pastor and his wife graciously received me and gave me a place to stay in their house. Although much progress had been made, the purely indigenous congregation still had never had a woman preacher. They were reluctant to have me now for this reason, but eventually relented, and I became, thus, the first woman to preach to their congregation.

When I entered the church, I was thrilled. Only a handful of them had received the Holy Ghost when I first came. Now there was a great multitude of spirit-filled believers in that place, and they were financially prosperous and had built, with their own resources, what must surely be the finest indigenous church in all of Ecuador. The architecture was superb, and the building was clean and well-maintained.

I was sorry that my Spanish was not better, for I had a burning message on my heart. The people were patient with my limited vocabulary and seemed to catch with enthusiasm what I was sharing with them. I spoke of the end-time things and made sure they knew that God wanted them to love and help the Jews (which now lived visibly among them).

I left Otavalo, pleased that God had indeed heard my prayers on behalf of those people and traveled back to the capital on a late-night bus, mindful of the fact that my plane was to depart early the next morning. I was trusting God to get me there safely, and He did.

Leaving Quito was a bittersweet experience. We wept on each other's shoulders, not knowing when we would see each other again. As always, our parting was made less bitter by the knowledge that we surely would meet one day, whether here or There.

Less than a year had passed when I was there again, just before Christmas, this time with a group organized by my pastor from the camp in Ashland. Twenty-five of us had come this time for a stadium crusade in the capital city. The crowds were wonderful and the anointing was wonderful, and God did great things in our midst.

Many people came into the capital from other towns, among them some of my Indians from Otavalo. What a blessing to see them again! And what a joy it was to rejoice together in the services!

Great crowds were saved and baptized in the Holy Ghost, many miracles of healing took place, and a sizable offering was received and left with the pastor for a new church building. We left with a sense that no man can alter the plan that God has for Ecuador and its people.

Brazil

My love for Brazil has never diminished. As God had appeared to me twenty-one years before in my room and first told me to go there, now He began to speak to me to return. Prophecies came forth in the church and from those who are close to me. The Lord told me that things would not be the same as they had been before in Brazil, that the same people would not necessarily be in the same places, but that He was taking me back to a different group of people.

My pastor saw in the Spirit that the burden for Brazil had lighted upon a dear sister who had come down from her home in the New York City area for some meetings at the camp. Her name was Virginia Brown. When I told Virginia what the Lord had shown us and that I wanted her to accompany me on the trip, she was delighted. From the very beginning her burden was equal to mine. Travel plans went smoothly, and within a week we were on our way.

This trip was indeed different. Instead of traveling widely around Brazil, as I had on the previous trip, we concentrated on ministering to a group of new churches in Rio de Janeiro, all founded within the last nine years. The group was made up of mostly young pastors and mostly young members. What an enthusiastic group! And how we loved them!

There was much praise and worship and dancing in the Spirit among these people. They love God and are totally committed to evangelism, to getting out and finding people wherever they are and winning them to the Lord. They go after the unchurched, even in the streets. They had us constantly on the go, as they whisked us here and there throughout the suburbs to more churches and meetings.

What wonderfully challenging messages God gave! I hadn't previously met anyone in this group, but now the Lord gave me exactly what was needed for every service and, during those days, we formed some wonderful friendships, never to be forgotten. After we had ministered to the people in the church, we ministered to the pastors in their homes. They were just as hungry as the people. As we laid hands on them and prophesied over them, we sensed the greatness of what God has in store for them in these last days.

I was able to see some of those we had known before. Some of them had grayer hair and some walked more haltingly, and several of them had lost their mates in the intervening years, but it was wonderful to see them all again. We rejoiced and wept together. Dear Sister Pessoa, who had been our hostess many years ago, was a widow now, but was continuing to serve the Lord faithfully in the Assemblies of God of Brazil. We were thrilled to see that this group has remained firm in doctrine and grand in scope, numbering nearly ten million members. With their emphasis on holiness of life and outreach to the community, they must surely be one of the finest national groups of churches anywhere in the world. They are always there when people need them.

We walked along the main strand at Cococabana, drank coconut milk, lifting our hands and thanking God for what He was doing in Brazil. We were there only three weeks this time, but God was able to do much in a short time. We came home happy, seeing that Brazil will be well represented in the Kingdom of Heaven.

Chapter 12

China

For thou hast girded me with strength unto the battle: thou hast subdued under me those that rose up against me. Psalm 18:39

As an artist and Christian, I had long had an interest in China. I loved Chinese art, especially the handwork: the enamels, the cloissoné, the lacquerware, the carved ivories and jades and soapstones. I studied textile design, illustration, sculpture and art history and literature for four full years at Moore Institute of Art in Philadelphia and loved the beautiful arts of China.

Growing up I had always seen Chinese art objects in our home. Then, as a child and as a teenager, I read for interminable hours the volumes of *National Geographic* magazines in my grandmother's library. I went to many museums where, again, I saw that many of this world's things of beauty came from China. Surely the calling for China was already being formed deep within me. This intense education put within me a desire to go there and see for myself.

I thus grew up with a deep appreciation for the land, for the people, and for the culture, as well as for the art of that land. There was, however, much more to it than that. I loved Jesus, and because I loved Jesus I had a burden for the souls of the people who, I knew, did not know Him. As my ministry developed, the fascination of sharing the Gospel with a people who had been cloistered for so long from social contact with the rest of the world seemed like an utterly wonderful prospect. When China began to open its doors to tourism, therefore, in 1980, a group of us from our church determined to be among the first to go in. Since then I have made about twenty trips into China.

From the very beginning we were amazed to see the sometimes total spiritual ignorance of Christ that existed inside China. Coming from a Christian land, where a multitude of churches, Sunday schools, special crusades and radio and television ministries all broadcast freely the love of Christ, it was hard to believe that many Chinese did not recognize the names of the Patriarchs of the Bible or even of Jesus Himself. Since China had no heritage of Christian ethics, we found their way of thinking to be totally different from our own.

In those first years anyone who wanted to go to China had to do so in an organized tour. To be known as "missionaries" there was totally unacceptable, and visa applicants were carefully screened. Travel had to be well-planned and well-supervised. To each foreign tour group there were assigned official guides. There was a national guide, who was with you from the moment you arrived in the country to the moment you departed. Aiding him or her in each place to oversee the activities of the group, were several local guides. The Soviet Union had employed this same system. It was a method of isolating tourists, keeping them away from the common people and seeing that they did not engage in any "subversive" activities — such as telling people about Jesus and the Bible. No deviation from the planned program or the state-approved itinerary was permitted.

I became very burdened for the souls of those guides, all of whom were trained Communist officials. They were deeply indoctrinated so that they would not be unduly influenced by foreigners. They received their positions because they were trusted to remain good Communists and to see that Communism was protected from the evil influences of the West.

At first, it seemed that we were very restricted. We could not freely give out literature. We could not openly and publicly preach the Gospel. We were kept as far away from the people as was possible. It became, for me, an intense burden, to believe for the salvation of those with whom we *could* come into contact, the guides themselves. Privately, we all began to pray for our guides. When one of them was not feeling well, we made it a point to pray for him openly in the name of Jesus.

One of the most important things we could do to win our guides was to live the Christian life before them. Because they had been denied access to foreigners for so many years, they were very interested in us and observed us carefully. It was a time to let our lights shine and to allow the beauty of the fruits of the Spirit to attract them to Christ.

As the ice began to break, we would go further. I, for example, would put my arm around the waist of a so-phisticated young lady guide, lead her around the statuary in a Chinese garden we were visiting as a group, and take the opportunity to speak to her from the depths of my heart about my faith in the Lord Jesus Christ. I spoke of His wonderful love and care for her, of the provision of His marvelous blood shed for her on the cross of Calvary, and of the Father's yearning over the Chinese people, that a large number of them would dwell with Him in Heaven throughout eternity.

"Because of His great love for you, the Chinese people," I told her, "there are more of you on the Earth than of any other race of people." It was delightful to see the effect this had upon her heart and soul. The Chinese are noted for hiding their emotions, but every year and in every visit, I have seen that stereotype cracked by the power of the Holy Ghost. His love is such a great force, and winning men and women to Christ is His work. We are just willing vessels which He uses to do that work.

What a joy to see that woman break and begin to weep! By the time we had reached the other side of the garden, she had already earnestly given her heart to the Lord Jesus Christ and entered into her first fledgling days of new life in Him.

As the guides were saved, we laid hands on them, explaining that the One who had saved them was now going to give them the gift of the Holy Ghost. They did have halting inquiries: would others know about this? What would happen to them? We assured them that God would hold them close and safeguard them from harm, and that it was totally up to them whom they told and when. Slowly, we taught them that God was able to show them how to speak to other people, just as we had spoken to them. To see the Light of Christ dawn in their souls was a wonderful experience.

Not every guide was receptive to our message. They had been well indoctrinated, and some opposed what we were telling them. In fear and hardness of heart, these pulled back. The old doctrines of Communism did not die easily, and the iron fist of control was not easily relaxed. Those guides who were saved immediately saw the difference between the spirit of those hardened men and women who rejected our witness and the members of our group.

When these people got saved, their hopes for the future soared like an eagle. To think that they would not be under the system of tyranny forever and that they could be free and happy was an exhilarating and heady experience for them and one that was thrilling to watch. It brought us great joy.

The level of freedom we have had to work for God openly in China has come and gone since that time with the political tides. For several years there was increasing openness. Then, after the famous Tienamen Square episode, things tightened up again. We never knew which trip might be our last. We were determined, therefore, to make the best of every opportunity and to hear the Lord say (one day when the doors are eventually shut tight), "When I was moving in China, you were there." Nothing could be more wonderful for the dedicated believer than to hear the Master say, "Well done!" That means everything to me.

On one of our trips into China many years ago, another sister and I had the privilege of speaking very late one night in the corridor of our hotel with a very highly placed guide, a young man of great authority in the party ranks. He was pouring out his heart to us there where no one else could overhear him and, with much help from Heaven, I was pressing upon him the claims of Christ.

"Can this Jesus forgive even someone who has killed Christians?" he asked, letting us know that he had been a member of some Red Guard unit that had been sent against believers to destroy them.

As I looked into his beseeching eyes, I could feel the

power of God running over me like warm oil and knew that he could see Christ in me. I knew that he could see Heaven in my face in that moment and sense that there was indeed a better life awaiting him.

"Yes!" I answered. "Jesus can and will forgive even that."

For a moment there was silence, as his soul hung in the balance. I am absolutely sure that the Lord tipped the scales His way and will continue to lead that young man and that one day I will see him *in that land that is fairer than day*.

How blessed I feel to have been so many times to China, to see the countryside, the unusual mountain formations, especially in Guilin where the tall, rocky mountains rise like sheer shapes from the landscape. To see the mists upon those mountains enabled me to understand the Chinese paintings I had seen in my art books and in museums.

As a person who loves to cook and who has enjoyed a variety of good restaurants in my years of growing up and living in the big city of Philadelphia, to see the cooking arts of China, the deliciously prepared fifteen-course meals, and the gardens that supplied the produce for such a feast, was a delight. In the West, we prefer chicken, but duck is the more desired for the Chinese. We saw flocks of white ducks floating on every stream and pond. As we traveled about by train and by bus, we saw that the Chinese must utilize every available bit of arable land to grow food for their masses of people. The seemingly unending rows of vegetable plots, with beans and cabbages and other vegetables, grow right up to the railroad right of way or the road.

Because family size has been limited for so long in

China, the Chinese people treasure their children and dote over them, educating them well and dressing them with the best they can afford. It has always brought us much joy to see China's children.

For each trip Brother Heflin was led of the Lord as to the particular cities to be visited and the itinerary to be followed. We tried to visit all parts of the country, and as we walked through the land from day to day, we prophesied over the land and over the people. Just our praises, filling the Chinese atmosphere, have had an impact. The Lord said to us, "I have taken your praises and your worship and blown them with the winds of My Spirit into every corner of China."

We have watched as Brother Heflin has prayed for the deaf and dumb in the shops and marketplaces and seen the light come to their faces as they were instantly healed.

We have crisscrossed the land, covering both the easy places and the difficult places, the near places and the far-flung places. We have gone to the mountains, the deserts, the valleys, the rivers, and the coastal canals and, as a result, the mighty hand of God has touched China and continues to touch China to bring forth a people fit for His glory. We have thus added our strength to the Chinese church, to all those who believe and who dwell in that great land.

We have prayed for unnumbered multitudes of people and seen them saved and filled with the Holy Ghost. Those who have received the Lord and whose lives have been saved from destruction, those who are now vessels for Him, have been strengthened and taught and healed and blessed and are the seed of the new China, the kindred which God speaks of who shall be represented in Heaven.

The Chinese church grows more powerful every day, filled with God's Spirit, and is a victorious church. Yes, it is a suffering church, but it is also an overcoming church, and we are caught up together in the blessed fellowship of His suffering in that victory with them. There could be no greater privilege in all the Earth!

Chapter 13

Afghanistan

*For by thee I have run through a troop; and by my
God have I leaped over a wall.*   Psalm 18:29

One of the most outstanding moves of God that I have
ever been privileged to witness took place in Afghanistan. The country, which lies just north of India and just
south of Russia, has for centuries been a place of mystery
and danger for outsiders; for the people of Afghanistan
are often warlike and, for the most part, fanatically Moslem.

Long before the Russian invasion of Afghanistan, the
Lord told us to go there as one stop on an around-the-
world ministry trip. We walked in the streets, meeting
people and ministering to them. We spoke to many and
prayed for them.

There, in the marketplace of Kabul, the Lord spoke to
me that He would use me to speak to the Jewish popula-
tion of the country. I had no idea how to begin contacting
the Jews in a country where many of them were in hiding
to protect their lives.

How should I go about finding them? Israel has many enemies around the world, and I do not speak of Jewish matters to anyone unless the Spirit of God gives me a special sign that it is safe to do so. That day, in the marketplace of Kabul, I saw the Spirit light upon a man and knew that I must speak with him. I sensed that the man was a Moslem, yet I knew that the Spirit of God was showing me that it was safe to speal with him.

"Do you know any Jewish people?" I asked.

His face lit up in a very friendly manner. I could see that he had a good spirit. "I do," he said, "I know the Rabbi and, if you want, I will take you to him tonight." I told my pastor what had happened, and he suggested that I take with me an Australian couple who were accompanying us on the trip.

True to his word, the man came to our hotel that night and took us in a car. We went up one street and over a hill and came to a long blank wall which seemed to surround a residence.

The Afghan sky was very dark that night as the man led us up to the door of the gate and knocked. Someone inside asked who was there. I spoke forth a Hebrew greeting, a greeting of peace and blessing. The door opened wide and someone said, "You may come in, but he (referring to the Moslem) must stay out." So our friend waited while we went inside.

We explained to those who had opened the door that we were in town for only a few days, that we would be leaving the next evening, but that God had given us a message for the Jewish community, and that we would like to see the Rabbi. It was Wednesday, and we were informed that many of the Jewish community would be gathered the following day in the synagogue to celebrate the sixth day of *Shavuot*. We could see the Rabbi there. We awaited that meeting with joy and anticipation.

The following day, Brother Heflin joined us and the four of us made our way to the synagogue. We were received warmly. They placed on Brother Heflin's head the yarmulke and around his shoulders the prayer shawl and asked him to preach. What a wonder! A Pentecostal preacher speaking in a Jewish synagogue in a Moslem country.

He was led to use prophetic scriptures from the Old Testament to speak to the people that day and to call them to worship and faith. The message of the hour, he told them, was for all Jews to go home to Israel. They listened with tear-streaked faces and later told us, "Many have already gone. Now, we will do our best to go also." In the Spirit, we warned them that a time of danger was coming.

That afternoon, as we walked in the streets of Kabul, another lady and I were led by the Spirit to speak with Jewish businessmen. In the evening, feeling that we had done what we could, we flew out of Kabul to continue our trip.

Two years later we felt led of the Lord to go to Afghanistan again. This time, things were heating up, and we were held in house arrest in Kandahar. To our surprise we saw the red wings of the Russian Air Force already painted on the doors at the Army air base there. We looked at each other, and a cold chill swept over us. We knew that this meant the Russians were coming and that it was too late to do anything more in Afghanistan than pray and prophesy.

That night we were kept in our rooms by an armed guard, and in the morning we were allowed to proceed to Kabul. There, unlike the previous trip, we were not permitted even to leave the airport and travel into the city. We had to stay right there until our flight out of the country left, so we spent our time praying and prophesying over the capital city.

Years before, when God wanted to move in Afghanistan, he raised up a Pentecostal woman and sent her there to teach the people. She was harassed and eventually shot in the back and killed. Once she was dead, the members of the church she had built were martyred and the building was leveled to the ground. Gleefully, the citizenry plowed up the land where the church building had been situated, looking for what they had been told was "an underground church."

The devil thought he had defeated the purposes of God in that land, but God does not take it lightly when His Church is persecuted. When the blood of the martyrs cries to Him from the ground, He moves in judgment. The Russians came down like a horde of vultures and occupied it for many bloody and brutal years. Not many people understand why, but there is always a *why* with God.

Even as judgment was imminent, God had given the Afghan people an opportunity to hear of His love. How could we have known of the terrible devastation that was to follow? We can only hope that now that the yoke of the Russian oppressor has been lifted the Afghans will, at last, turn to the true and living God and receive forgiveness. Let us pray that they will repent and allow the Church to flourish, so that there may be a people from Afghanistan in Heaven on *that day*.

Years later, in our many travels, we met an Afghani Jewish woman. We asked her what had become of the Jews in the Kabul Synagogue during the Russian occupation. She said some had been shot and killed.

With every news story, there is *the news behind the news*. I always think of that in connection with the Afghanistan story. My grandmother, who took many trips to the Caribbean, often told me when I was a child of the eruption of Mt. Peleé on the Island of Martinique at the turn of the century. She heard many stories about it when she was visiting there on vacation. The town at the base of Peleé was a pirate town, a wicked place, the Sodom and Gomorrah of its day. Ships from all over the world docked there, and the sailors came into town for wine and women and dancing and carousing.

One day, God spoke to a couple of missionaries in the United States to go there and preach Christ. They obeyed, preaching in the streets of the city, telling all of the sacrifice of Christ on Calvary's cross, of the power of His blood to cleanse from all sin, and about Heaven and Hell. To the last man, the town rejected their message, jeering and mocking the men.

It became a game with the townspeople to find devilish ways to torment and mock the visitors. One day they took a pig and put it on a crude cross they had made. In a drunken parade, they carried the crucified pig through the streets.

When they did that, God told the missionaries to hire a small boat and to row as far offshore as they could. When they had rowed a great distance from shore, they turned and looked back. Suddenly there was a rumbling. It was as if the fist of God had been plunged into the top of the mountain, a large crater appeared, and poisonous gasses spewed out in a cloud and totally covered the city. Even their boat had ashes in it.

When the two American missionaries went back into the city, they found the streets littered with dead bodies. Inside the shops they found more bodies. Inside the

houses they found more bodies. Of all the inhabitants of
the city, only one man survived. He had been imprisoned
in an underground room and, therefore, escaped the terrible tragedy.

I have never forgotten that story. Grandmother had not
told me the part about the missionaries or the fact that
what happened was the judgment of God. All she told me
was that a terrible tragedy had occurred in which forty-
four thousand people lost their lives in one day. Many
years later I got *the news behind the news* from a Christian
publication that came from California.

Chapter 14

Conclusion

*It is God that girdeth me with strength, and maketh
my way perfect.*   Psalm 18:32

God holds the great plan for everything. He has a plan
for *your* life. He wants *you* to come to Him and give yourself to Him unreservedly, so He might have the pleasure
of using you to the fullest.

As I said at the outset, the pages of the Bible are filled
with the stories of men and women in both ordinary and
extraordinary feats. The common denominator of all is
that each of them was ordinary until he or she was
touched by God. That touch made them extraordinary.

If it had not been for those visitations from the Lord,
when He came to me in my days of loneliness, disap-
pointment and crisis, I would never have had the joy of
going to the nations for Him, and my life would have
been lived, no doubt, in selfishness and self-pity. How
very different my story would have been! And, because
of it, other's lives would have been different too.

I am grateful for His tenderness, His compassion, and
His great love for me! Who am I that He has visited me?

Without Him there would have been no victory, no fruit and no life. He is to be greatly praised.

Not every moment of my time is spent in overseas ministry. I preach the Word of God at Calvary Pentecostal Tabernacle in Ashland and at our church in Richmond, Virginia. Our camp activities and administration require a lot of my time and attention, too. Aside from this ministry, the Lord has allowed me to participate in some wonderful revivals in America. Among them, two stand out in my mind.

Fort Wayne, Indiana

In Fort Wayne, Indiana, about two hundred people from various church backgrounds were meeting in someone's living room. They were not accustomed to women preachers, but the Lord impressed upon the pastor of the group to invite me for revival, and what revival we had!

Charismatic families came, heard and were laid out on the floor under the power of God. The prophetic word searched out the hearts of the people.

We had such great victory and so many lives were turned upside down during those days that ten of the people went with us to Russia that year. One family moved to Israel, although they were not Jewish, and have lived there ever since.

Sanford, North Carolina

Sanford, North Carolina was another of those cities that received revival. I have preached in towns all over North Carolina. I always enjoy it, for it is part of America's Bible Belt, and people there are hungry for the Lord and respond well to the Gospel.

In Sanford, a pastor and his wife, who owned a Christian bookstore, invited me to come for revival. Because of their work in the bookstore, they knew all the other pastors in town. After all, they were his clients, so he was on good terms with them. He felt that God would use these good contacts to bless many people. Someone told him that it was not time, that the church was too young, but he chose to listen to the Lord instead.

I had been fasting for twenty-one days on only water when I got his call, and knew that it was God's time for Sanford.

Each night, the pastor and his wife led the worship service, and I preached. There was a heavy presence of God in the place, a glory cloud. The prophetic word went forth like a sword, changing many lives for all eternity. During those days many people made the decision to go into full-time service for the Lord.

There was something very odd about the services. It seemed like we had two altar calls every night. In the first, many members were blessed, healed of long-standing diseases, and filled with the Spirit. Later, after their own church services would be over, other pastors would come with hungry hearts to receive more. They made up the second altar call. Folks laid on their faces for hours.

During the daytime, people who had attended at night would come and spend time with us in the bookstore, just wanting to be near us, hungering to receive more. As we talked, some wept and some fell under the power of God there among the book racks.

This glory of God wafted out over the city, and we felt it everywhere we went. When I went into a store to buy some stockings or some other personal item, I laid my Bible on the counter and would soon notice that the clerk was weeping. Through the word of knowledge, the Lord would have me tell her that she had known the Lord when she was younger, but that now He was calling her to Himself again, and that is what she was feeling. There and then, she would give her heart to Jesus. Many sales people and bank tellers were saved during those days of revival.

Toward the end of the week, a local pastor gave me the opportunity to preach on his radio program and the glory spread over the town.

After only one week of meetings, ten people came from Sanford to camp to serve the Lord full-time, and many of them became wonderful preachers and missionaries.

How many more nations are there yet to be visited? What new experiences does tomorrow hold? What pleasures will knowing Him better each day produce? Only God knows, but tomorrow is more wonderful than today. I love Him more than ever and am more ready than ever to serve Him. With ever increasing joy and expectation, I look forward to the days just before His coming, for the nations I will visit, for the people that I will meet and minister to, for the ones I will embrace in His name and for those who will stand with me in Heaven on that glory shore. Together, we shall behold Him throughout eternity.

Come to the Lord today and seek Him with all your heart. When He speaks to you, answer joyfully and quickly, "Yes, Lord," and when He moves, you will have the joy of beholding His face and being in partnership with God in His work in the Earth.

To listen to His voice and say "Amen" means that you will have His message, His anointing, His presence and His financing. You will have a glorious place in this life and in the eternal life to come.

Unto Him be the glory, both now and forever.

Amen!

For thou wilt light my candle: the Lord my God will enlighten my darkness.

For by thee I have run through a troop; and by my God have I leaped over a wall.

As for God, his way is perfect: the word of the Lord is tried: he is a buckler to all those that trust in him.

For who is God save the Lord? or who is a rock save our God?

***It is God that GIRDETH ME WITH STRENGTH**, and maketh my way perfect.*   Psalm 18:28-32

Notes

Notes

ℭ𝔰 *Notes* 𝔰𝔬

Notes

❧ Notes ☙

Ministry address:

Rev. Viola Weidemann
11352 Heflin Lane
Ashland, Virginia 23005